WRITING

SAT Study Guide

PASS
YOUR
SAT

© 2014 Breely Crush Publishing, LLC

971041214143

Published by Breely Crush Publishing, LLC
10808 River Front Parkway
South Jordan, UT 84095
www.breelycrushpublishing.com

ISBN–10: 1-61433-481-1
ISBN–13: 978-1-61433-481-1

Printed and bound in the United States of America.

*SAT is a registered trademark of the College Board and its affiliated companies, and does not endorse this book.

Table of Contents

Section 1: Identifying Sentence Errors

USING WORDS CORRECTLY

The most fundamental element of a sentence is the words. Words are the basis of all writing. It is often how words are used, rather than which words are used, that makes writing particularly persuasive or interesting. However, it is most important to first ensure that the words are being used correctly. Below some of the most commonly misused words are defined.

There - is used to refer to a location
Their - is used to show possession or ownership
They're - is the contraction for "they are"

WRONG: John was certain he had parked the car in the third row, but it was not **their**.

CORRECT: John was certain he had parked the car in the third row, but it was not **there**.

WRONG: **They're** candy uses some of the most high-quality ingredients in the world.

CORRECT: **Their** candy uses some of the most high-quality ingredients in the world.

WRONG: **There** going to the store after lunch, so the girls needed to grab **they're** purses.

CORRECT: **They're** going to the store after lunch, so the girls needed to grab **their** purses.

Its - is a pronoun (i.e., it is used in place of a previously identified noun)
It's - is the contraction for "it is"

WRONG: The car's battery was **it's** oldest part.
CORRECT: The car's battery was **its** oldest part.

WRONG: **Its** just not true that Samantha stole the money.
CORRECT: **It's** just not true that Samantha stole the money.

Were - is the past tense state of being
Where - is used to indicate location

WRONG:	Jennifer asked her mother **were** she was going later.
CORRECT:	Jennifer asked her mother **where** she was going later.

WRONG:	Kelly's manager informed her that they **where** going to have a meeting, and told her **were** it would be.
CORRECT:	Kelly's manager informed her that they **were** going to have a meeting, and told her **where** it would be.

Compliment - is used to describe a nice comment directed towards another person
Complement - is used to describe something which adds to or completes something else

WRONG:	Wanting to flatter her boss, Mary **complemented** his new suit.
CORRECT:	Wanting to flatter her boss, Mary **complimented** his new suit.

WRONG:	The interior designer felt that the yellow pillows **complimented** the purple drapes perfectly, and that they added a nice brightness to the room.
CORRECT:	The interior designer felt that the yellow pillows **complemented** the purple drapes perfectly, and that they added a nice brightness to the room.

Affect - means to influence
Effect - indicates a result

WRONG:	Jared decided that he would not let his co-worker's jealousy **effect** him.
CORRECT:	Jared decided that he would not let his co-worker's jealousy **affect** him.

WRONG:	The **affect** of the Civil War was the abolition of slavery.
CORRECT:	The **effect** of the Civil war was the abolition of slavery.

Then - indicates order in a sequence, or the result of an action
Than - is used to make comparisons

WRONG:	Anna woke up, did her hair, and **than** went to the store.
CORRECT:	Anna woke up, did her hair, and **then** went to the store.

WRONG:	The supervisor believed that she was much smarter **then** the manager.
CORRECT:	The supervisor believed that she was much smarter **than** the manager.

Accept - indicates agreement or receiving something
Except - indicates something which is not included

WRONG:	Consuelo was nervous, and she worried that her fiancé's family would not **except** her.
CORRECT:	Consuelo was nervous, and she worried that her fiancé's family would not **accept** her.

WRONG:	All of the flowers, **accept** the red ones, should be placed in vases on the tables.
CORRECT:	All of the flowers, **except** the red ones, should be placed in vases on the tables.

Ensure - indicates assurance and means to guarantee
Insure - refers to insurance coverage

WRONG:	The private detective **insured** the client that their spouse was not cheating on them.
CORRECT:	The private detective **ensured** the client that their spouse was not cheating on them.

WRONG:	The insurance agent assured the man that he was **ensured** in the case of a fire.
CORRECT:	The insurance agent assured the man that he was **insured** in the case of a fire.

Principal - is the leader of a school
Principle - is a standard, an initial investment

WRONG:	The teacher sent Molly to the **principle** because she colored on the wall.
CORRECT:	The teacher sent Molly to the **principal** because she colored on the wall.

WRONG:	The **principal** of honesty is an important one in the service industry.
CORRECT:	The **principle** of honesty is an important one in the service industry.

Capitol - a building where politicians or lawmakers meet
Capital - an amount of money, an uppercase letter, a city, or a synonym of "excellent."

WRONG:	Congress was required to meet in the **capital** that morning.
CORRECT:	Congress was required to meet in the **Capitol** that morning.
WRONG:	The firm's investment of **capitol** was all lost when the stock market crashed.
CORRECT:	The firm's investment of **capital** was all lost when the stock market crashed.
WRONG:	The class took a field trip to the **capital** building in the capitol city of Des Moines.
CORRECT:	The class took a field trip to the **Capitol** building in the capital city of Des Moines.

Farther - refers to an increase in actual, physical distance
Further - more, or refers to relative distances

WRONG:	Jennifer asked how much **further** it was to the post office.
CORRECT:	Jennifer asked how much **farther** it was to the post office.
WRONG:	If you annoy me **farther** then I will not drive this car any further, and we will not make it to the party on time.
CORRECT:	If you annoy me **further** then I will not drive this car any farther, and we will not make it to the party on time.

Precede - to go before something
Proceed - to continue

WRONG:	The mayor's float **proceeded** the fire station's float in the parade.
CORRECT:	The mayor's float **preceded** the fire station's float in the parade.
WRONG:	After the jury had calmed down the judge told the witness to **precede**.
CORRECT:	After the jury had calmed down the judge told the witness to **proceed**.

Lay - an incomplete verb which requires a direct object, and it refers to setting something somewhere
Lie - an untruth, or a complete verb meaning to recline (i.e., subjects lie down, they lay things down).

| WRONG: | Sandra decided to **lie** down after a long day at work. |
| CORRECT: | Sandra decided to **lay** down after a long day at work. |

| WRONG: | Courtney had to **lay** the check on the counter while she looked for her keys. |
| CORRECT: | Courtney had to **lie** the check on the counter while she looked for her keys. |

i.e. - used to demonstrate "that is"
e.g. - used to demonstrate "for example"

| WRONG: | Kendra went to her least favorite place that day; **e.g.,** the dentist. |
| CORRECT: | Kendra went to her least favorite place that day; **i.e.,** the dentist. |

| WRONG: | The manager told her to take classes that would improve her skill set; **i.e.,** typing, spreadsheets, or webpage design. |
| CORRECT: | The manager told her to take classes that would improve her skill set; **e.g.,** typing, spreadsheets, or webpage design. |

Loose - the opposite of tight
Lose - the opposite of win

| WRONG: | Daryl took the shirt back to the store to exchange it for a smaller size because it was too **lose**. |
| CORRECT: | Daryl took the shirt back to the store to exchange it for a smaller size because it was too **loose**. |

| WRONG: | John would not make the bet with his brother because he was too afraid to **loose**. |
| CORRECT: | John would not make the bet with his brother because he was too afraid to **lose**. |

Council - a group of people
Counsel - advice

| WRONG: | The city **counsel** was meeting to determine the tax rates for the next year. |
| CORRECT: | The city **council** was meeting to determine the tax rates for the next year. |

| WRONG: | The board sought the **council** of the accountant before changing their policy. |
| CORRECT: | The board sought the **counsel** of the accountant before changing their policy. |

WHAT IS A SENTENCE?

A sentence is a cohesive expression of an idea. Sentences are built using different combinations of clauses and phrases.

<u>Phrase</u>: A group of related words, but which DOES NOT have its own subject and verb.

> "After going to the store" is a phrase. It does express a thought, but it does not have a subject.
> "from California" is a phrase. It does not have a verb or a subject.

<u>Clause</u>: A group of related words which DOES have its own subject and verb. There are two different levels of clauses: independent clauses and dependent clauses.

<u>Independent Clause</u>: A clause that can stand on its own. It conveys a complete idea.

<u>Dependent Clause</u>: A clause that cannot stand on its own. It does not convey a complete idea.

> "She went to the store" is an independent clause. It has a subject, "she," a verb, "went," and conveys a complete thought.

> "When the dog barks" is a dependent clause. It has a subject, "dog," and a verb, "barks." However, it does not convey a complete thought. Rather, it requires additional phrases or clauses to complete its meaning.

Phrases and clauses can be combined to create sentences. There are essentially four different types of sentences:

- Simple sentences = One independent clause
- Compound sentences = Two independent clauses
- Complex sentences = One independent and one dependent clause
- Compound-complex sentences = At least two independent clauses and one dependent clause

The dog swam across the pond. This is a simple sentence. It is composed of a single independent clause.

Lucy played pinball at the party, and Jake flirted with the girls. This is a compound sentence. It contains two independent clauses, "Lucy played pinball at the party" and "Jake flirted with the girls."

While we were eating, the waitresses cleaned the kitchen, but the busboys relaxed outside.

> Independent clauses – "the waitresses cleaned the kitchen" and "the busboys relaxed outside"
> Dependent clause – "While we were eating"
> So, it is a compound-complex sentence.

After going to the store, I ate pie. This is a simple sentence. Although it may look like it contains two clauses because of the comma, it is actually a combination of a phrase and a clause.

Phrase – "After going to the store" contains no subject.

> Independent clause – "I ate pie" has a subject and verb and expresses a complete idea.

I will go to the store, or you will go. This is a complex sentence.

Dependent clause – "or you will go"

> Independent clause – "I will go to the store"

HINT: Sometimes it can be difficult to identify the difference between a compound and a complex sentence. One simple way to tell is that compound sentences will always contain coordinating conjunctions, and complex sentences will contain subordinating conjunctions.

Coordinating Conjunctions: There are only seven coordinating conjunctions. These are words which join ideas that are of equal strength. The seven coordinating conjunctions are for, and, nor, but, or, yet, so. These can be remembered with the mnemonic FANBOYS.

> **F**or
> **A**nd
> **N**or
> **B**ut
> **O**r
> **Y**et
> **S**o

Subordinating Conjunctions: These are all other ways of joining sentences that are not coordinating conjunctions. The use of a subordinating conjunction indicates that the two clauses are not of equal importance, or that one is dependent. A few examples of subordinating conjunctions are given below. This is not an exhaustive list of subordinating conjunctions. Many additional subordinating conjunctions also exist.

- Because
- Although
- Even though
- Despite
- If
- Unless
- Wherever
- After
- Before
- Since
- While
- Until

There are many errors which can be made in sentence construction, the most common of which are described below.

Comma Splice: Possibly the common most error in writing, a comma splice occurs when two complete sentences are fused together with a comma. Just remember this: a comma can never, ever, hold two complete sentences together by itself. At the very least a coordinating conjunction is needed. Below are examples of sentences containing a comma splice:

> I can't go to school today, I will go tomorrow.
> The dog just ran into the street, he was running when he was hit by a car.
> Eat your sandwich, then take a bath.

Run-On Sentences: The "run-on" or fused sentence is simply two sentences put together without appropriate punctuation in between. If there are two parts to a sentence and both parts can stand alone, there must be appropriate "breaking" apart of the sentences. The following example illustrates this error.

> "Love means many different things to many people it's hard to give a distinct definition of it."

Notice that the above word grouping contains TWO subjects and TWO verbs: "Love means many different things to many people" / "It's hard to give a distinct definition of it."

Sentence Fragments: A "fragment" is incomplete. It is a word grouping that lacks a subject, a verb, or a sense of completeness.

> *I know he didn't commit the crime. Because he was at the movies.* The second sentence here is a fragment because is consists of a single, dependent clause. "Because he was at the movies" does not demonstrate a complete thought.

> *The boy, swimming in the ocean.* This sentence is a fragment because it contains no verb. Without a helping verb along with it "swimming" is not a verb.

> *She had lots of health problems.* Like an irregular heartbeat and migraine headaches. The second sentence here is a fragment because it lacks a subject.

Fragments often occur because the writer is dependent on the sentence previous to the fragment to complete the idea; however, in academic writing, you must not write in conversational fragments. Each word grouping must be a complete sentence. If a clause starts with a subordinating word like because, it cannot stand by itself and must be combined with an independent clause.

Subject – Verb Agreement: One of the most fundamental aspects of creating cohesive sentences is that the subject and verb need to be in agreement. In other words, singular subjects require singular verbs, and plural subjects require plural verbs. This tends to be fairly instinctual, but can sometimes become confusing.

SUBJECT – VERB AGREEMENT

If a teacher tells you that you have an agreement problem, he/she is NOT talking about a conflict. That instructor is using a common term to point out that two items are not "in sync" with each other.

1. Subject-Verb Agreement: If a teacher tells you that you have an agreement problem, then you'll need to look at the subject of your sentence and the verb of your sentence.

   a. Subjects and Verb Must Match in Number:
   It may seem strange, but even verbs are singular or plural, and in English, the singular verbs usually end in –s. The subject and the verb must BOTH be plural or BOTH be singular:

   Singular: **He swims** in the pool.
   Plural: **They swim** in the pool.

The most common error is in not recognizing whether a subject is singular or plural. Many errors occur because a student doesn't know that the following words (indefinite pronouns) always take a singular verb:
Another / any / anybody / anyone / anything / each / either / everybody / everyone / everything / much / neither / nobody / no one / nothing / one / other / somebody / someone / something.

The "-body," "-one," and "-thing" words always take the singular even if they "sound" plural, like "everybody," or "everything."

Everybody knows that the world is round.
Everyone looks beautiful in the glow of candlelight.
Everything tastes delicious.

b. Compound subjects take plural verbs:
The **corn, peas, and carrots are** homegrown.
Cussing and swearing remain a problem in the public buildings of our nation.

c. If the word "each" or "every" occurs before a subject joined by the word "and," then the verb becomes singular:
Every man and woman on this earth **has** a mother.

d. If two subjects are joined by the word "or," or "nor," the verb agrees with the part closer to the verb.
Neither the cat nor the two dogs are properly groomed.
Neither the two dogs nor the cat is properly groomed.

2. Pronoun-Antecedent Agreement: This error occurs when the pronoun of the sentence doesn't match its antecedents. Pronouns can be either singular or plural.

The boys and girls fought to maintain their independence from their parents.
Every horse and mule runs at its own pace.
Every student in the room ran to pick up **his/her** bookbag.

TIP: Beware the use of the pronoun "their." One of the most common errors is a problem with subject-pronoun agreement. For instance, a student might write, "A parent loves their child." The instructor would mark that as an error because "A parent" is one person. The pronoun "their" is a plural word, and therefore the two don't agree. The correct sentence would have both pronoun and its antecedent either singular in number:

A parent loves his/her children. (singular)
OR
Parents love their children. (plural)
If the his/her – he/she construction seems awkward and intrusive, then switch both subject and pronoun to the plural.

3. Pronoun Shift: Once you begin an essay or paper, be consistent with the pronouns you use. If you start out using the pronoun "one," then don't switch midway through the paper to the pronoun "he," or "you."

If **one** wants to travel, then **he** should start saving money now.
If **one** wants to travel, then **one** should start saving money now.
OR
If **he** wants to travel, then **he** should start saving money now.

TIP: Some instructors don't allow the use of the informal "you" in college-level papers. Be sure you have a full understanding of the expectations of this particular professor before you turn in your paper.

4. Tense Shift: Present tense is something happening right NOW. Past tense is something that has happened before now, and future is something that WILL happen. Once you begin a sentence, keep the tenses consistent unless you intentionally mean to show a difference in time.

Patricia **laughed and cried** until she **falls** asleep. WRONG!
Patricia **laughed and cried** until she **fell** asleep. RIGHT!

5. It is also important to make sure that all subjects and pronouns agree in terms of gender. If the subject of a sentence is male, all pronouns must be masculine. If the subject of a sentence is female, all pronouns must be female.

WRONG: **Jeremy** gave the dogs a treat and put them in the back of **its** car.
CORRECT: **Jeremy** gave the dogs a treat and put them in the back of **his** car.

WRONG: **Sally** went to get **her** purse so that **he** could pay the hairdresser.
CORRECT: **Sally** went to get **her** purse so that **she** could pay the hairdresser.

NOT PREFERRED: The **firemen** were very strict in **their** schedules.
CORRECT: The **firefighters** were very strict in **their** schedules.

6. Also be sure to use the relative pronouns who, that, and which appropriately.

    Who should refer to people.
    That should refer to things, groups, and important clauses.
    Which should refer to groups, things, and nonessential clauses.

WRONG:	The mayor told the people **that** were there to vacate the premises.
CORRECT:	The mayor told the people **who** were there to vacate the premises.

WRONG:	The dog **who** kept barking was taken by animal control.
CORRECT:	The dog **that** kept barking was taken by animal control.

WRONG:	It was Jane's decision that the car, **that** was old, should be impounded.
CORRECT:	It was Jane's decision that the car, **which** was old, should be impounded.

7. Ensure that pronouns always have a clear reference.

    UNCLEAR:
    Jane and her mother had an argument. She told her that the job was a bad idea.
    The use of pronouns to describe Jane and her mother makes the second sentence unclear.

    CORRECT:
    Jane and her mother had an argument. Her mother told her that the job was a bad idea.
    Jane and her mother had an argument. She told Jane that the job was a bad idea.
    Either of these revisions is acceptable and greatly clarifies the second sentence.

TENSE

The term tense refers to when something happens. It is important to make sure that all of the verbs in a sentence are in the correct tense, otherwise the sentence will not make sense and will not properly express the idea. There are six different tenses.

	Past Tense	Past-Perfect Tense	Present Tense	Present-Perfect Tense	Future Tense	Future-Perfect Tense
Being verb	I was	I had been	I am	I have been	I will be	I will have been
Irregular verb	I slept	I had slept	I sleep	I have slept	I will sleep	I will have slept
Regular verb	I worked	I had worked	I work	I have worked	I will work	I will have worked

<u>Past Tense</u>: The past tense is used when something has happened already.

> *Jordan **was** a member of the band in high school.* This sentence indicates that Jordan played a band instrument in the past. It is a description of an event which took place and was completed.

> *Sheryl and Ashley **slept** in until 3 p.m. the day after the party.* This sentence indicates that the two girls on some unspecified day in the past did not wake up until 3 p.m. The sentence describes an event which was completed.

> *Erika **worked** until the project was finished.* This sentence indicates that Erika was doing work in the past, but that now it is completed.

<u>Past-Perfect Tense</u>: The past-perfect tense is used to describe something which occurred in the past. In other words, it describes something which "passed in the past." It combines the helping verb "had" with the past tense form of the verb.

> *Jordan **had been** a member of the band in high school.* This sentence indicates that Jordan played a band instrument in the past. Further, it indicates that this is no longer the case, and the event has been completed.

> *Sheryl and Ashely **had slept** until 3 p.m. the day after the party.* This sentence indicates that the two girls on some unspecified day in the past did not wake up until 3 p.m. It further implies that this is not normal, and is not typically expected.

> *Erika **had worked** until the project was finished.* This sentence indicates that Erika was doing work in the past. However, the project is completed and she is now not working.

Present Tense: The present tense describes something which happens in the present. This is the most basic form of the verb.

*Jordan **is** a member of the high school band.* This sentence indicates that currently Jordan is attending high school and is part of the band. This is an ongoing truth and is still the case.

*Sheryl and Ashley **sleep** until 3 p.m. the day after the party.* This sentence is a statement of fact. It is a current truth, and is not completed or over.

*Erika **works** until the project is finished.* This sentence indicates that Erika is currently working. It implies that she has been working and that she will continue working until whatever project she is a part of is completed.

Tip: There are two common mistakes using the present tense:

#1: Be sure that when you are describing a relatively permanent truth, you use the present tense form of verbs.

WRONG:	I have always believed that the church **was** true.
CORRECT:	I have always believed that the church **is** true.

WRONG:	The newspaper article **was** scathing in its review of the play.
CORRECT:	The newspaper article **is** scathing in its review of the play.

#2: When an **infinitive** follows a verb in the <u>past or past-perfect tense</u>, shift it to the present tense.

WRONG:	We would <u>have liked</u> **to have eaten** the meal, but there was no time.
CORRECT:	We would <u>have liked</u> to *eat* the meal, but there was no time.

WRONG:	He <u>wanted</u> **to have gone** to the game, but he had to work.
CORRECT:	He <u>wanted</u> to *go* to the game, but he had to work.

Present-Perfect Tense: The present-perfect tense is used in a number of situations. It is often used with the words "for" and "since." It is also used if an action has been completed, but a mentioned time frame has not. It is also used when something is very recent.

*Jordan **has been** a member of the high school band.* This indicates that Jordan is currently a member of the band and joined the band some time ago.

*Ashley and Sheryl **have slept** until 3 p.m. the day after the party.* This sentence indicates that Ashley and Sheryl have awoken, but the "day after the party" has not ended (i.e., it is the day after the party). Likely, the two girls have just awoken recently.

*Erika **has worked** until the project was completed.* This sentence indicates that Erika has just finishing working on the project.

Future Tense: The future tense is used when something is going to happen in the future. It is formed using "will" and the present tense form of the verb.

*Jordan **will be** a member of the band in high school.* This sentence indicates that Jordan is not yet attending high school, nor is he a member of the band. However, it is certain that this will be the case in the future.

*Ashley and Sheryl **will sleep** until 3 p.m. the day after the party.* This sentence indicates that the party has not occurred, and the two girls have not gone to sleep. However, it is certain that after the party they will not awake until 3 p.m. the next day.

*Erika **will work** until the project is completed.* This sentence indicates that the project has not been completed. However, there is no doubt that Erika will continue working until it is completed.

Future-Perfect Tense: The future-perfect tense talks about the past in the future. In other words, it is used to refer to an action that will be completed in the future In other words, it describes something which will soon be in the past, or which will "have" happened. It is formed by combining the helping verb "will have" with the past tense form of the verb.

*Jordan **will have been** a member of the band in high school.* This sentence indicates that Jordan is not yet a member of the high school band, but it anticipates a future day when this event will have passed. Essentially it is speaking as though the future has occurred already.

*Ashley and Sheryl **will have slept** until 3 p.m. the day after the party.* This sentence indicates that the two girls will sleep in the day after the party. This has not occurred yet. Rather, it is expected that it will occur and anticipates it having passed.

*Erika **will have worked** until the project is completed.* This sentence indicates that Erika has not completed work on her project. However, at some point in the future she will have completed it and it will then be a past event.

MODIFIERS

Much of writing consists of using modifiers to clarify and describe other words. The two types of modifiers are adjectives and adverbs.

Adjectives are words that modify (describe, limit, clarify, etc.) nouns, pronouns, or subjects. They are descriptive words.

*The carpenter refinished the **worn** countertop.* In this sentence, the word worn identifies additional information about the countertop. Therefore, it is an adjective.

*Her daughter is **qualified** to do her taxes.* In this sentence, the word qualified describes the pronoun her. Therefore, it is an adjective.

Adverbs are words that modify verbs, adjectives, and other adverbs. Essentially rather than providing descriptive information about something, they provide descriptive information about how something is done. Often adverbs end in "ly."

*After completing her morning walk **briskly**, Samantha quickly showered.* The word briskly is an adverb because it modifies the verb completing. The word quickly is an adverb because it modifies the verb showered.

In the following sentences **adjectives are bolded** and <u>adverbs are underlined</u>.

The **black** and **white** dog <u>quickly</u> ran after the <u>slowly</u> moving **ice cream** truck.
The **tall** man walked <u>very slowly</u> back to his **small**, **dingy** office.
Samantha was <u>extremely</u> **glad** that she would be able to attend **baseball** camp.

Some of the most common mistakes made with modifiers are described below:

<u>Dangling Modifiers</u>: These occur when an introductory phrase tells of an action, but the subject of the sentence is not the performer of the action.

Sobbing inconsolably, the teacher informed the student that she could not raise his grade. In this sentence, the introductory phrase "sobbing inconsolably" is meant to describe the student. However, the teacher is identified first. Therefore, it is a dangling modifier.

Incorrect use of modifiers: Remember that most adverbs end in "ly." Real is an adjective, whereas really is an adverb. Also, surely is an adverb, but sure is not. Be certain that you are correctly using modifiers.

WRONG: You did real good in the basketball game.
CORRECT: You did really well in the basketball game.

WRONG: He was sure happy that she said yes.
CORRECT: He was surely happy that she said yes.

CASE/ POINT OF VIEW

SHIFT IN POINT OF VIEW

When you write, you may opt to use the *first person point-of-view,* I or we.

The *second person point-of-view* is using "you." (Before you utilize the word "you," addressing the reader on an informal basis, clarify with your instructor whether or not he/she allows that kind of informality.)

The *third person point-of-view* means using the pronouns, "he, she, it, or they."

Whatever point-of-view you choose, be consistent.

"The entire continuum of care exists under one roof. A leader in cancer education, the Cancer Center has served the area for more than a decade. The Center has a full staff of registered doctors and nurses to aid our patients. We have a special treatment room where you can watch television as your chemotherapy is being delivered. The staff is caring and compassionate, and they are all Board Certified. "

Notice the inconsistencies between the use of the point of view from "the Cancer Center" (it) to "we," and "they," as well as the switch from the word "patients" to "you." Pick a point-of-view and stick with it!

In addition to point of view, case is another important factor in writing. There are three different cases that are used in writing. They are the subjective case, the objective case, and the possessive case. The appropriate pronoun to use is based on which case the pronoun occupies.

	1st person singular	1st person plural	2nd person	3rd person singular	3rd person plural	Relative
Subjective	I	We	You	He, she, it	They	Who, which, that what, whatever, whoever
Objective	Me	Us	You	Him, her, it	Them	Whom, whomever, which, whichever
Possessive	My, mine	Our, ours	Your, your	His, her, hers, its	Their, theirs	whose

Subjective Case: This is used when the pronoun is referring to the subject of the sentence. Also use the subjective case to complete the meaning of being verbs.

WRONG: *Jane asked if **her** could go to the store.* The pronoun "her" is referring to the subject of the sentence, Jane. Therefore, it incorrectly uses the objective case.

CORRECT: *Jane asked if **she** could go to the store.* The pronoun "she" is referring to the subject of the sentence, Jane. Therefore, it correct uses the subjective case.

WRONG: *Samantha told the manager that **it was her** who shredded the files.* The objective case is incorrectly used in this sentence because it is supposed to refer to the subject. As written, Samantha is telling the manager what the manager did.

CORRECT: *Samantha told the manager that **it was she** who shredded the files.* The subjective case is correctly used in this sentence because it completes the being verb "it was."

Objective Case: The objective case is used when the pronoun is referring to the object of a sentence, rather than the subject. The object is the item or noun in the sentence which the verb is acting on, or which receives the benefit of the action.

WRONG: *You can ship the package to Jordan or **I**.* The pronoun "I" is incorrect in this context because it a subjective pronoun; however, it occupies an objective position.

CORRECT: *You can ship the package to Jordan or **me**.* The pronoun "me" is the correct use of the objective form. "Me" is the object because it receives the benefit of the verb "can ship."

WRONG: *The teacher returned Sally's report to* **she** *after it had been graded.* The subjective pronoun is used incorrectly in this sentence. The pronoun occupies an objective position.

CORRECT: *The teacher returned Sally's report to* **her** *after it had been graded.* The objective pronoun her is used correctly in this sentence. "Her" is objective because it is receiving the benefit of the verb "returned."

Possessive Case: This is used to denote ownership or possession. The most common way to indicate possession is adding an " 's " to the end of a noun or pronoun or to use any of the possessive pronouns.

WRONG: *Sally bought the diagram. The diagram was* **she's**. Here the subjective pronoun "she" is incorrectly used in a possessive position.

CORRECT: *Sally bought the diagram. The diagram was* **hers**. Here the possessive pronoun "hers" is used correctly. Notice that the possessive pronouns do NOT have an apostrophe in them. This is also true of the possessive pronouns his, its, ours, theirs, and yours.

WRONG: *The* **companies** *stock price plummeted after the death of the CEO.* Here the plural form of company is incorrectly used in place of the possessive form of the word.

CORRECT: *The* **company's** *stock price plummeted after the death of the CEO.* Here the possessive form of company is used by adding an apostrophe and s to the end of the word.

Additional Guidelines for Possessive Words:

1. If something is owned by multiple individuals, show possession by adding an apostrophe after the plural form of the word.

WRONG: *The* **girl's** *room was always a mess.* This indicates that there is a single girl and her room was always messy.

CORRECT: *The* **girls'** *room was always a mess.* Indicates that two or more girls share a single room, and it is always messy.

2. If there are multiple individuals that possess an item, simply add an " 's " after the plural form of the word.

WRONG: *The* **child's** *school was immaculate.* This would indicate that the school was attended by a single child.

CORRECT: *The* **children's** *school was immaculate.* Indicates that there are many children who attend the school, and it is clean.

3. To derive the possessive form of a plural word ending in s (such as when multiple individuals own a single item), simply add an apostrophe.

WRONG: *The **Johnsons** have a nice car.* This does not indicate possession.

CORRECT: *The **Johnsons'** have a nice car.* This indicates that there are multiple people in the Johnson's family and they own a nice car.

4. When listing multiple owners of a single item, only change the final owner to the possessive case.

WRONG: ***Beth's and Derik's** house is very small.* This indicates that Beth and Derik each own their own house, and that each of their houses is small.

CORRECT: ***Beth and Derik's** house is very small.* This indicates that Beth and Derik own the house together.

5. When listing the owners of multiple items, change each owner to the possessive case.

WRONG: ***Beth and Derik's** houses are very small.* This indicates that Beth and Derik own the houses together.

CORRECT: ***Beth's and Derik's** houses are very small.* This indicates that Beth and Derik each own their own house, and that each of their houses is small.

Sample Questions – Test Yourself

Identify the sentence error or if there is no error, mark it as (E) No Error.

1. Often *(A) <u>the subject of poetry and song</u> a full moon, *(B) <u>has been blamed</u> for the howling of dogs, the thirst *(C) <u>of vampires</u>, the advent of lunacy, and *(D) <u>increasing births</u>. *(E) <u>No Error</u>

2. *(A) <u>Relaxing with a cold drink</u> and *(B) <u>lying</u> on the beach in my bikini, *(C) <u>the dog</u> startled me when he barked *(D) <u>loudly</u>. *(E) <u>No Error</u>

3. *(A) <u>While the crowds at an airport</u> illustrate the diversity *(B) <u>of people</u>, they also *(C) <u>emphasized</u> the *(D) <u>universality</u> of human nature. *(E) <u>No Error</u>

4. *(A) <u>A subtle delight</u> builds in me *(B) <u>as I smear the soap</u> over the slick metal and *(C) <u>lather up</u> the car that takes me *(D) <u>anywhere and everywhere</u> I want to go. *(E) <u>No Error</u>

5. *(A) <u>When the frost</u> is on the pumpkin, one has to *(B) <u>don gloves</u>, or *(C) <u>he</u> will get *(D) <u>very cold fingers</u>. *(E) <u>No Error</u>

6. *(A) <u>Every person</u> in the store ran to claim *(B) <u>their</u> free ice cream when *(C) <u>the bonus prize was announced</u> over the *(D) <u>loudspeaker</u>. *(E) <u>No Error</u>

7. *(A) <u>When</u> the young immigrant woman *(B) <u>arrived</u> by jet *(C) <u>on the United States</u>, she went *(D) <u>directly</u> to Washington, D.C. *(E) <u>No Error</u>

8. *(A) <u>The pastry chef</u> thought she *(B) <u>was losing her mind</u> because she couldn't *(C) <u>remember if the</u> chocolate cake and the strawberry pie *(D) <u>was in the oven</u>. *(E) <u>No Error</u>

9. An old proverb *(A) <u>says</u> that if one *(B) <u>lives</u> in a glass house, *(C) <u>he</u> should *(D) <u>not</u> throw stones. *(E) <u>No Error</u>

10. The man was *(A) <u>better-looking</u> than her brother, *(B) <u>smarter than</u> her father, *(C) <u>as rich as</u> her uncle, and *(D) <u>nicer than</u> her grandmother. *(E) <u>No Error</u>

SAMPLE QUESTION KEY – TEST YOURSELF

1. D
2. C
3. C
4. E
5. C
6. B
7. C
8. D
9. C
10. E

SECTION 1: IDENTIFYING SENTENCE ERRORS QUESTIONS

Identify the sentence error or if there is no error, mark it as (E) No Error.

1. Jennika informed the police that *(A) <u>she had seen</u> the suspect *(B) <u>take out</u> a wrench, *(C) <u>break the</u> window, and *(D) <u>then started sneaking</u> into the house. *(E) No Error

The correct answer is D:) then started sneaking. This part of the sentence is not parallel with the rest. It should read "and sneak into."

2. The secretary *(A) <u>quickly</u> signed *(B) <u>the documents,</u> *(C) <u>they were</u> going to *(D) <u>be late</u> to a meeting. *(E) <u>No Error</u>

The correct answer is C:) they were. This is a dangling modifier because the subject "they" following the modifying statement.

3. Sam informed *(A) <u>his only</u> lawyer, *(B) <u>and no one</u> else, that *(C) <u>he was going</u> to be out of town *(D) <u>for the week</u>. *(E) <u>No Error</u>

The correct answer is A:) his only. The modifier "only" is misplaced. As stated it indicates that he has only one lawyer, when it is meant to state that he told not one but his lawyer. It should read "only his."

4. The manager *(A) <u>decided that</u> it would be easier for all of the firm's partners to fly to *(B) <u>colorado</u> for their meeting *(C) <u>than</u> it would be *(D) <u>for them to fly</u> to Hawaii. *(E) <u>No Error</u>

The correct answer is C:) colorado. Colorado is a proper noun and should be capitalized like Hawaii.

5. *(A) <u>Sarah worried</u> that her dog would *(B) <u>not be fed</u> if she went out of town, so *(C) <u>she decided</u> to take *(D) <u>them</u> to a kennel. *(E) <u>No Error</u>

The correct answer is D:) them. Them is a plural noun and is being used to refer to the singular dog. It should be changed to "it."

6. Jane's *(A) <u>father insisted</u> that they could not take *(B) <u>all of her pets</u> on vacation; *(C) <u>rather</u>, they *(D) <u>could take either</u> the dogs or take the cats. *(E) <u>No Error</u>

The correct answer is D:) could take either. In order for the clause to be parallel it should read "could either take."

7. *(A) <u>It is</u> common for *(B) <u>the CEO</u> of a company *(C) <u>to take</u> great pride in *(D) <u>their</u> work. *(E) <u>No Error</u>

The correct answer is D:) their. There should be used to refer to plural nouns, but CEO is singular. It should be "it" instead.

8. Erik *(A) <u>complemented</u> his sister *(B) <u>on</u> her new hairstyle, *(C) <u>and told</u> her that *(D) <u>he thought</u> it suited her. *(E) <u>No Error</u>

The correct answer is A:) complemented. Comple*e*mented is used incorrectly here. It should be compl*i*mented.

9. Jared *(A) <u>assured his</u> boss that his new girlfriend would not *(B) <u>effect</u> his ability to work, *(C) <u>and insisted</u> that he *(D) <u>was perfectly able</u> to concentrate. *(E) <u>No Error</u>

The correct answer is B:) effect. *E*ffect is used incorrectly here. It should be "*a*ffect."

10. The assistant manager *(A) <u>could not</u> figure out why the computer system *(B) <u>wasn't running</u> properly: *(C) <u>it's</u> calibration had *(D) <u>just been</u> set the previous day. *(E) <u>No Error</u>

The correct answer is C:) it's. "It's" is the contraction for "it is" and is used incorrectly in this context. Instead it should be "its."

11. *(A) <u>The witness pled</u> with the jury *(B) <u>to release</u> the defendant because *(C) <u>he</u> couldn't have *(D) <u>committed</u> the crime. *(E) <u>No Error</u>

The correct answer is E:) No Error. All of the verbs correctly use the past tense.

12. To become *(A) <u>a fireman</u> is the *(B) <u>goal of</u> most of *(C) <u>the children</u> in *(D) <u>the kindergarten class</u>. *(E) <u>No Error</u>

The correct answer is A:) a fireman. The neutral form "firefighter" should be used instead.

13. *(A) <u>The detectives</u> were confounded by the case because *(B) <u>their lead</u> suspect was on television at *(C) <u>the time of</u> the murder. *(D) <u>Its</u> impossible for him to have been in both places at once. *(E) <u>No Error</u>

The correct answer is D:) Its. The contraction "it's" should be used instead of the pronoun "its."

14. Audrey *(A) <u>decided that</u> even though *(B) <u>she needed</u> $15.00 she would *(C) <u>only ask</u> her mom *(D) <u>for</u> $10.00. *(E) <u>No Error</u>

The correct answer is C:) only ask. The modifier "only" is misplaced. It is meant to modify "her mom," not "ask."

15. The *(A) <u>bank employee</u> was *(B) <u>real</u> good at his job, *(C) <u>but the manager</u> did not *(D) <u>choose him</u> for a promotion. *(E) <u>No Error</u>

The correct answer is B:) real. "Real" is used incorrectly. It should be the adverb form really.

16. I *(A) <u>needed</u> a drink of water, *(B) <u>so I decided</u> to go *(C) <u>to the</u> fridge and get *(D) <u>us</u> one. *(E) <u>No Error</u>

The correct answer is D:) us. The tense of the rest of the line is first person singular and "us" is second person plural.

17. The *(A) <u>receptionist admitted</u> that it was *(B) <u>her</u> who answered *(C) <u>the phone</u> when the manager *(D) <u>called</u>. *(E) <u>No Error</u>

The correct answer is B:) her. The subjective case "she" should be used rather than the objective "her."

18. *(A) <u>Anthony's</u> teacher *(B) <u>asked</u> if *(C) <u>Joshua and him</u> would *(D) <u>give</u> the first report. *(E) <u>No Error</u>

The correct answer is C:) Joshua and him. While it is correct to list Joshua's name first, "he" should be used instead of "him."

19. *(A) <u>After the party,</u> *(B) <u>Jane and I</u> went *(C) <u>home to</u> go to *(D) <u>sleep</u>. *(E) <u>No Error</u>

The correct answer is E:) No Error. All of the verbs and subjects are in the correct tenses and cases.

20. The *(A) <u>teacher apologized</u> that *(B) <u>he could</u> not lead the club *(C) <u>meeting</u> because *(D) <u>their time</u> was too important. *(E) No Error

The correct answer is D:) their time. "Their" is the incorrect reference for the singular subject teacher. His, her, or some neutral reference should be used.

21. *(A) <u>Jordan and me</u> decided to go *(B) <u>to the store</u> and buy *(C) <u>some milk</u> to have *(D) <u>with</u> the cookies. *(E) <u>No Error</u>

The correct answer is A:) Jordan and me. The subjective form I should be used instead of the objective form me.

22. *(A) <u>Both</u> the teacher or the administrator *(B) <u>had to be</u> present *(C) <u>when</u> the students *(D) <u>were at</u> recess. *(E) <u>No Error</u>

The correct answer is A:) Both. Because the sentence indicates that the teacher or the administrator must be present, it would be more logical to begin the sentence with "either."

23. *(A) <u>The new product</u> was scheduled to *(B) <u>be introduced</u> to the *(C) <u>market</u> on *(D) <u>Wednesday</u>. *(E) <u>No Error</u>

The correct answer is E:) No Error. The verbs are all in the correct tenses.

24. *(A) <u>Angie was</u> planning to go *(B) <u>not only</u> to China, *(C) <u>but</u> to *(D) <u>Singapore</u>. *(E) <u>No Error</u>

The correct answer is C:) but. The sentence is indicating that both China and Singapore are Angie's intended destinations. Therefore, the line should read "but also" rather than "but."

25. *(A) <u>The</u> letter *(B) <u>which</u> she put in the mailbox *(C) <u>was a birthday</u> card for *(D) <u>her mother</u>. *(E) <u>No Error</u>

The correct answer is B:) which. The letter should be referred to as "that" rather than "which" because "she put in the mailbox" is important in identifying the letter.

26. The team *(A) <u>that</u> won the tournament *(B) <u>was very excited</u> to move on to *(C) <u>nationals</u> the *(D) <u>next week</u>. *(E) <u>No Error</u>

The correct answer is A:) that. Teams are referred to with "which," not "that."

27. The *(A) <u>couple was</u> arguing *(B) <u>and yelling</u> and *(C) <u>throwed</u> dishes against *(D) <u>the wall</u>. *(E) <u>No Error</u>

The correct answer is C:) throwed. The past-tense form of throw is threw, not throwed.

28. *(A) If one wishes to travel *(B) then it is important *(C) to ensure that *(D) their passport is up to date. *(E) No Error

The correct answer is D:) their passport. In order for the tense to be parallel through the sentence the underlined portion should appear "one's passport."

29. Each *(A) of the millions of books *(B) in the Library of Congress *(C) is given a *(D) titles. *(E) No Error

The correct answer is D:) titles. The subjects of the sentence – "each" and "is" – are both singular. Therefore, "title" should be used rather than "titles."

30. *(A) The receptionist asked *(B) who she *(C) was supposed to give the *(D) message to. *(E) No Error

The correct answer is E:) No Error. The verbs are all in the same tense, and nouns and references are all in agreement.

31. *(A) Me gave *(B) a copy of the *(C) book to the editor *(D) for review. *(E) No Error

The correct answer is A:) Me. The subjective form "I" should be used rather than the objective form "me" because answer A is being used to identify the subject of the line.

32. *(A) Finish your chores, *(B) then we can *(C) go to the park and *(D) play on the swing set. *(E) No Error

The correct answer is B:) then. A comma cannot be used to join to sentences without a conjunction. "And then" should be used rather than simply "then."

33. As I was *(A) considering the revisions *(B) which needed to be made, *(C) my managers, Mr. Jones, startled me when *(D) he walked into the room suddenly. *(E) No Error

The correct answer is C:) my managers. The singular form "manager" should be used rather than the plural. "Mr. Jones," and "he" are both singular subjects.

34. *(A) Another of the *(B) reason for the manager's decision to cut salaries was that *(C) profits had been down for *(D) the past three quarters. *(E) No Error

The correct answer is B:) reason. The plural "reasons" should be used rather than the singular "reason" because the sentence introduces an additional reason, indicating that there is more than one.

35. *(A) <u>Samantha</u> and *(B) <u>Jennifer's</u> computers *(C) <u>both having</u> problems *(D) <u>with</u> the screen resolution. *(E) <u>No Error</u> [*Assume that Samantha and Jennifer each own their own computer*]

The correct answer is A:) Samantha. If Samantha and Jennifer each own their own computer then each should be referred to separately. The line should read "Samantha's and Jennifer's computers."

36. *(A) <u>Even though</u> the jury *(B) <u>did not believe</u> him, the defendant *(C) <u>insisted</u> that *(D) <u>he had rode</u> the train to the bus station the day before. *(E) <u>No Error</u>

The correct answer is D:) he had rode. The correct form of the verb "ride" which should be used in the sentence is "ridden."

37. During *(A) <u>times when</u> I have had a lot of stress *(B) <u>in my life</u>, I *(C) <u>had written</u> stories *(D) <u>to cheer myself</u> up.*(E) <u>No Error</u>

The correct answer is C:) had written. The rest of the sentence uses the present-perfect tense (it says "have had") not the past-perfect tense ("had written"). Therefore, the present-perfect form "have written" should be used.

38. The *(A) <u>dog was</u> smarter, *(B) <u>faster</u>, and *(C) <u>was more clean</u> than the *(D) <u>other dogs</u> in the competition. *(E) <u>No Error</u>

The correct answer is C:) was more clean. In order for the sentence to have parallel construction the underlined portion should appear "cleaner."

39. *(A) <u>After going</u> to the *(B) job <u>interview</u>, the man *(C) <u>was sure that</u> it was the right job *(D) <u>for him</u>. *(E) <u>No Error</u>

The correct answer is E:) No Error. All of the correct references are used.

40. *(A) <u>Because of</u> the extreme darkness, the people all *(B) <u>beginned</u> to *(C) <u>scream</u> in *(D) <u>fear and confusion</u>. *(E) <u>No Error</u>

The correct answer is B:) beginned. The correct past tense form of "begin" is "began."

41. Mckensi *(A) <u>told her friends</u> that she *(B) <u>was going to</u> take *(C) <u>Math and German</u> the next year *(D) <u>in school</u>. *(E) <u>No Error</u>

The correct answer is C:) Math and German. Because "Math" is used in a general sense rather than a specific sense, it should not be capitalized.

42. The traffic officer *(A) <u>told</u> Jennifer that she should drive *(B) <u>North</u> until *(C) <u>she found</u> the visitor *(D) <u>parking lots</u>. *(E) <u>No Error</u>

The correct answer is B:) North. Directions should only be capitalized if they are referring to a specific region rather than a general direction.

43. *(A) <u>I wish</u> that I had gone to the dance when I found out that all of my *(B) <u>friends had gone</u>, and they *(C) <u>had all had</u> a really fun time *(D) <u>there</u>. *(E) <u>No Error</u>

The correct answer is A:) I wish. The rest of the sentence is in the past tense. The line should read "I wished" rather than "I wish."

44. She was *(A) <u>however</u> the *(B) <u>greatest</u> musician *(C) <u>that the instructor</u> had ever *(D) <u>encountered</u>. *(E) <u>No Error</u>

The correct answer is A:) however. "However" is an interrupting element to the sentence and should be framed with commas.

45. John's mother *(A) <u>told him that</u> she was proud *(B) <u>of him</u>, *(C) <u>and that</u> he did very *(D) <u>good</u> in his soccer game. *(E) <u>No Error</u>

The correct answer is D:) good. "Good" is used incorrectly. It should be "well" instead.

46. *(A) <u>The engine in</u> *(B) <u>Mark's car</u> was *(C) <u>more reliable</u> than *(D) <u>Bryce's</u>. *(E) <u>No Error</u>

The correct answer is C:) more reliable. In order for the comparison to have parallel construction the segment should read "the engine in Bryce's car."

47. The teacher *(A) <u>graded</u> papers, and *(B) <u>than</u> she went home for the day *(C) <u>to take</u> care of *(D) <u>her family</u>. *(E) <u>No Error</u>

The correct answer is B:) than. The passage is indicating sequence, not a comparison. Therefore, "then" should be used rather than "than."

48. The supervisor *(A) <u>was going</u> to take *(B) <u>a few days</u> off to go *(C) <u>in</u> vacation *(D) <u>to Florida</u> the next weekend. *(E) <u>No Error</u>

The correct answer is C:) in. "On" should be used instead of "in."

49. David *(A) <u>was not sure</u> that his *(B) <u>sister was guilty</u>; *(C) <u>however</u>, she *(D) <u>confessed</u> to the crime. *(E) <u>No Error</u>

The correct answer is E:) No Error. The passage makes correct use of a semicolon, and all of the verbs agree in tense.

50. *(A) <u>The teacher asked</u> the students *(B) <u>whether or not</u> they wanted *(C) <u>to go to</u> the planetarium for a *(D) <u>field trip?</u> *(E) <u>No Error</u>

The correct answer is D:) field trip. The statement is declarative, not a question. Although the word "whether" is used, it is still not appropriate for a question mark to close the sentence.

51. People *(A) <u>who hike</u> the Appalachian Trail *(B) <u>may stay</u> *(C) <u>overnight</u> in shelters if *(D) <u>you</u> choose. *(E) <u>No Error</u>

The correct answer is D:) you. The rest of the sentence is written in third person, referring to "people who hike." You should not be used in this sentence because it is a second-person reference.

52. *(A) <u>College Professor #11</u> *(B) <u>teaches</u> *(C) <u>their children</u> to write *(D) <u>biographies</u>. *(E) <u>No Error</u>

The correct answer is C:) their children. College Professor #11, though not named, is a single individual. Therefore, it is improper for the plural reference "their" to be used. Instead, either his, her, or a neutral reference should be used.

53. His son *(A) <u>grew up</u> *(B) <u>to become</u> a successful doctor, author, soccer *(C) <u>coach, and</u> have *(D) <u>a very successful</u> family life. *(E) <u>No Error</u>

The correct answer is D:) a very successful. This element is not parallel with the rest of the sentence which is composed of single word nouns ("author," "soccer," etc.).

54. *(A) <u>My mother was</u> a very special woman *(B) <u>with extraordinary talents</u> *(C) <u>who made</u> a comfortable home *(D) <u>and was</u> a gracious host. *(E) <u>No Error</u>

The correct answer is E:) No Error. The verbs are all in the same tense and the line is punctuated correctly.

55. *(A) <u>Convinced that</u> our *(B) <u>community</u> was not *(C) <u>well informed</u> about the issues, *(D) <u>pamphlets were printed</u> about the program. *(E) <u>No Error</u>

The correct answer is D:) pamphlets were printed. The first part of the sentence is an introductory phrase, and because it does not describe the words "pamphlets were printed" the result is a misplaced modifier which confuses the meaning of the sentence.

56. *(A) <u>Cindy asked</u> her *(B) <u>mother how</u> much *(C) <u>further</u> it *(D) <u>was to the</u> store. *(E) No Error

The correct answer is C:) further. The sentence is referring to an actual, physical distance. Therefore, father should be used rather than further.

57. Jeremy *(A) <u>insured</u> his mother that *(B) <u>he had every</u> intention of *(C) <u>doing his homework</u> after the *(D) <u>party</u>. *(E) <u>No Error</u>

The correct answer is A:) insured. The word "insured" should only be used when referring to insurance coverage. In this context, the word "ensured" should be used instead.

58. *(A) <u>I can't go</u> to the *(B) <u>store, I will</u> go *(C) <u>after I finish</u> reading this *(D) <u>article</u>. *(E) <u>No Error</u>

The correct answer is B:) store, I will. This sentence is composed of two independent clauses. It therefore requires a coordinating conjunction after the comma, and without one the sentence is a comma splice.

59. Dr. Smith *(A) <u>cannot attend</u> the conference tomorrow, *(B) <u>but he will go</u> the next day after *(C) <u>he finished</u> the *(D) <u>necessary</u> paperwork. *(E) <u>No Error</u>

The correct answer is C:) he finished. The sentence is referring to a future event. The past tense "finished" is therefore used incorrectly.

60. *(A) <u>It was Jane's</u> decision *(B) <u>that</u> the car, *(C) <u>which was old</u>, should *(D) <u>be impounded</u>. *(E) <u>No Error</u>

The correct answer is E:) No Error. That and which are both used properly in this sentence.

61. Sam *(A) <u>and Aaron</u> argued *(B) <u>fervently</u>. *(C) <u>He told him</u> not to speak *(D) <u>to the detective</u>. *(E) <u>No Error</u>

The correct answer is C:) He told him. Because both Sam and Aaron are male, the two references "he" and "him" are unclear.

62. *(A) John's mother told *(B) him that it was a *(C) well decision for him *(D) to go to college. *(E) No Error

The correct answer is C:) well decision for. "Well" is used incorrectly in this context. "Good" should be used instead.

63. Isabella agreed that *(A) she car *(B) really needed to *(C) be taken to the mechanic later *(D) that day. *(E) No Error

The correct answer is A:) she. The pronoun should be in the objective case because it is referring to the car, not the subject Isabella. The objective "her" should be used rather than "she."

64. *(A) Everybody that *(B) were at the fundraiser *(C) donated money to the *(D) children's hospital. *(E) No Error

The correct answer is B:) were. Were is the plural form of the verb; however, everybody is a singular subject. Therefore the correct verb to use is was.

65. The hotel guest *(A) was shocked to learn that his room *(B) had not been cleaned, *(C) and he asked *(D) to who he should complain. *(E) No Error

The correct answer is D:) to who. This portion of the sentence is meant to inquire as to the object of the sentence, not the subject. Therefore the objective "to whom" should be used.

66. Kenneth *(A) assured the officer that *(B) he had purchased the car two months ago *(C) and that it was *(D) hims. *(E) No Error

The correct answer is D:) hims. "Hims" is not a proper reference. Also, the reference should be singular. Therefore "his" should be used instead.

67. Consuelo felt that *(A) Tonio's family did not *(B) except her, and she *(C) felt awkward when *(D) she was around them. *(E) No Error

The correct answer is B:) except. Except is used to identify exclusions to a general rule. The sentence requires a word which means approval. Therefore "accept" should be used instead.

68. When Columbus *(A) <u>sailed</u> from Spain in 1492 he *(B) <u>was</u> actually looking for a passage to India. When he reached America he *(C) <u>assumed</u> he had been successful and *(D) <u>had called</u> the native people Indians. *(E) <u>No Error</u>

The correct answer is D:) had called. The rest of the sentence is written in the past tense, but "had called" is the past perfect. Therefore, the element is not parallel.

69. Mass *(A) <u>transit,</u> or public transportation, refers to transportation systems which *(B) <u>are</u> available to the general public. *(C) <u>Including;</u> busses, trams, *(D) <u>subways,</u> <u>and</u> other such transportation systems. *(E) <u>No Error</u>

The correct answer is C:) Including. The semicolon is used improperly here. It is used to connect two clauses, and "including" is not a clause. No punctuation is needed here.

70. Fossil *(A) <u>fuels account</u> for about *(B) <u>88 percent</u> of energy *(C) <u>consumption</u> in the *(D) <u>United States</u>. *(E) <u>No Error</u>

The correct answer is E:) No Error. All of the terms are in agreement, and "88 percent" follows the correct rules of numbers.

71. The *(A) <u>Krebs cycle,</u> also called the citric acid cycle, *(B) <u>is the</u> process through which a cell *(C) <u>converted</u> carbohydrates, *(D) <u>fats, and</u> proteins into energy. *(E) <u>No</u> <u>Error</u>

The correct answer is C:) converted. The rest of the sentence is in the present tense, yet this is in the past. Therefore, the present tense "converts" should be used instead.

72. *(A) <u>The dogs</u> collar was *(B) <u>too small</u> for his neck, *(C) <u>and it did</u> not fit *(D) <u>him</u> comfortably. *(E) <u>No Error</u>

The correct answer is A:) The dogs. "Dogs" should be in the possessive because it is labeling the collar as belonging to the dog. Therefore, the correct form is "dog's."

73. *(A) <u>Marie's and Amber's</u> apartment *(B) <u>was on</u> the second *(C) <u>floor of a small</u> building just *(D) <u>off of the</u> main road. *(E) <u>No Error</u>

The correct answer is A:) Marie's and Amber's. There is only one apartment which is owned (or rented) by the two girls. Therefore, only the second subject, Amber, needs to be in the possessive.

74. *(A) <u>Jennifer was</u> *(B) <u>certain, she</u> went to *(C) <u>the police to tell</u> them who *(D) <u>had stolen</u> her car. *(E) <u>No Error</u>

The correct answer is B:) certain, she. This line has two clauses. The comma is not a correct way to combine two clauses; therefore, this is a comma splice.

75. *(A) <u>I know that</u> the manager *(B) <u>is</u> to blame *(C) <u>for</u> the spilled coffee. *(D) <u>Because he did it</u>. *(E) <u>No Error</u>

The correct answer is D:) Because he did it. This is a sentence fragment. It contains a single dependent clause which cannot stand as its own sentence.

76. She *(A) <u>was</u> *(B) <u>head over heels</u> in love with him, *(C) <u>so she</u> was willing *(D) <u>to forgive</u> his flaws. *(E) <u>No Error</u>

The correct answer is B:) head over heels. This is an idiom, and idioms should not be used in formal writing.

77. The boy *(A) <u>was swim</u> in the *(B) <u>ocean</u> when *(C) <u>he heard</u> the *(D) <u>lifeguard's</u> whistle blow. *(E) <u>No Error</u>

The correct answer is A:) was swim. The gerund form of swim, or swimming, should be used instead to reflect that the event is still occurring.

78. *(A) <u>Kevin was</u> quite *(B) <u>impressed</u> by *(C) <u>Amber; he</u> asked her to dance *(D) <u>timidly</u>. *(E) <u>No Error</u>

The correct answer is D:) timidly. This is an example of a misplaced modifier. Modifiers should be near the elements that they modify. In this case it should be near "he" not "dance."

79. This *(A) <u>winter</u> I am going *(B) <u>only</u> to Times *(C) <u>Square, and</u> to no *(D) <u>other</u> places. *(E) <u>No Error</u>

The correct answer is E:) No Error. The modifier "only" is properly used, and the elements are all parallel with each other.

80. *(A) <u>Not only</u> did *(B) <u>Natalie apply at</u> the state college, *(C) <u>but</u> at the *(D) <u>university</u>. *(E) <u>No Error</u>

The correct answer is C:) but. In order for the line to have parallel structure "but also" should be used in conjunction with the phrase "not only" which begins the sentence.

81. *(A) <u>I'm giving</u> the *(B) <u>grandfather</u> clock to my *(C) <u>grandmother</u> *(D) <u>with a broken face</u>. *(E) <u>No Error</u>

The correct answer is D:) with a broken face. This modifying phrase should be place near "grandfather clock" which it is meant to describe not "grandmother." Because it is not near the proper phrase, the sentence is unclear.

82. *(A) <u>Either</u> the *(B) <u>dog,</u> the *(C) <u>cat,</u> the mouse, or *(D) <u>the one snake</u> must have eaten the gerbil. *(E) <u>No Error</u>

The correct answer is D:) the one snake. This element is not parallel with the remaining animals which are listed.

83. *(A) <u>I am going</u> to the store *(B) <u>tomorrow</u> because yesterday *(C) <u>I will not have had</u> time *(D) <u>to</u>. *(E) <u>No Error</u>

The correct answer is C:) I will not have had. "Yesterday" is in the past. Therefore the past tense "I did not have" should be used instead.

84. The *(A) <u>newspapers</u> article about *(B) <u>sanitation was</u> really a shocking *(C) <u>exposition</u> about *(D) <u>school janitors</u>. *(E) <u>No Error</u>

The correct answer is A:) newspapers. The possessive form "newspaper's" should be used instead to indicate that the article was in the newspaper, rather than that there are multiple papers.

85. Janis *(A) <u>would have</u> liked *(B) <u>to have gone</u> to the conference, *(C) <u>but the company</u> could not afford *(D) <u>to send</u> her. *(E) <u>No Error</u>

The correct answer is B:) to have gone. Because the phrase "would have liked" appears first, "to have gone" should be converted to the present tense.

86. The *(A) <u>six foot</u> tall doctors *(B) <u>towered</u> over the *(C) <u>other members</u> of *(D) <u>the medical team</u>. *(E) <u>No Error</u>

The correct answer is A:) six foot. Because "six" and "foot" are adjectives that work jointly to describe the doctors, a hyphen should be used between them to clarify.

87. *(A) <u>Having heard</u> that her sister *(B) <u>was</u> sick, Mckensi *(C) <u>called</u> her to see if she *(D) <u>was feeling good</u> yet. *(E) <u>No Error</u>

The correct answer is D:) was feeling good. The word "good" is used incorrectly in this sentence "Well" should be used instead.

88. The *(A) <u>manager asked</u> if *(B) <u>Marcus and me</u> would *(C) <u>be willing</u> to take the *(D) <u>night shift</u> over the holiday. *(E) <u>No Error</u>

The correct answer is B:) Marcus and me. The objective "me" is used incorrectly here. It should be "Marcus and I" instead.

89. *(A) <u>The captain informed</u> the detectives *(B) <u>that he expected</u> an *(C) <u>up-to-date</u> report on his desk *(D) <u>first thing</u> in the morning. *(E) <u>No Error</u>

The correct answer is E:) No Error. The verbs are all in the proper tenses, and hyphens are all used correctly.

90. Samantha's *(A) <u>supervisor asked</u> her *(B) <u>whether</u> the calendar was *(C) <u>up-to-date</u> or not, and told her to *(D) <u>schedule</u> a company meeting for the next day. *(E) <u>No Error</u>

The correct answer is C:) up-to-date. Because up to date appears after the noun calendar, it does not require hyphens.

91. The police officer *(A) <u>asked</u> the girls *(B) <u>who's</u> fault the collision *(C) <u>was</u> so that he could *(D) <u>make</u> a formal report on the matter. *(E) <u>No Error</u>

The correct answer is B:) who's. Who's is used incorrectly in this sentence. It should be "whose" instead.

92. The *(A) <u>companies</u> insurance *(B) <u>would not cover</u> the *(C) <u>accident, even</u> though it involved the *(D) <u>company car</u>. *(E) <u>No Error</u>

The correct answer is A:) companies. This is the plural form of the word company, but what is required is the possessive form. The correct word for this sentence is company's.

93. The *(A) <u>Smiths'</u> shiny new *(B) <u>car</u> is the *(C) <u>envy</u> of the whole *(D) <u>neighborhood</u>. *(E) <u>No Error</u>

The correct answer is E:) No Error. The correct possessive form of Smiths is used, and all of the verbs are in the correct tense.

94. *(A) <u>The street</u> was dimly *(B) <u>lit, and</u> Sarah *(C) <u>was not sure</u> if the *(D) <u>mans'</u> badge was real or not. *(E) <u>No Error</u>

The correct answer is D:) mans'. The correct possessive form of man for this context is man's.

95. The *(A) Johnsons' car was *(B) shinier, *(C) newer, *(D) and had a nicer color than Angie's. *(E) No Error

The correct answer is D:) and had a nicer color. This element is not parallel with the rest of the sentence. The phrasing would have to be something like "nicer looking."

96. Bethany *(A) could not be certain that she would pass the *(B) class, however, she *(C) had done very well *(D) on the final. *(E) No Error

The correct answer is B:) class, however. In this sentence "however" is not an interrupting element, but the beginning of a new clause. Therefore, a semicolon should be used rather than a comma.

97. *(A) Shortly after *(B) getting a flu *(C) shot; Jon came down with *(D) a nasty case of the flu. *(E) No Error

The correct answer is C:) shot; Jon. The semicolon is incorrectly used to divide an introductory phrase from the main clause. The correct punctuation in this sentence would be a comma.

98. Wanting to appear *(A) self sufficient, Kendra was *(B) too proud to ask *(C) her parents for money *(D) after she had been robbed. *(E) No Error

The correct answer is A:) self sufficient. Whenever "self" is used as a prefix (except with selfish) a hyphen should be used to divide it from the root word.

99. *(A) Neither the jet *(B) or the airplane *(C) has been filled with gas in the *(D) past two weeks. *(E) No Error

The correct answer is B:) or. In order for the comparison to have parallel construction, "nor" should be used rather than "or."

100. *(A) Although Sam was shorter *(B) than his brother *(C) Jon, he was taller *(D) then his sister Sally. *(E) No Error

The correct answer is D:) then. This sentence is a comparison, not a sequence of events. Therefore, "than" should be used instead of "then."

101. The *(A) principal reason for *(B) his investment in the stock market *(C) was to save for *(D) his retirement. *(E) No Error

The correct answer is A:) principal. This spelling of the world principal is used to refer to the head of a school. Principle would be the correct word for this context.

102. *(A) <u>Jon went</u> to *(B) <u>the store</u> to *(C) <u>buy</u> a pack of cards. *(D) <u>Went to the library too</u>. *(E) <u>No Error</u>

The correct answer is D:) Went to the library too. This is a sentence fragment because it contains no subject.

103. *(A) <u>One should</u> always *(B) <u>check in with one's boss</u> before *(C) <u>you</u> spend *(D) <u>company money</u>. *(E) <u>No Error</u>

The correct answer is C:) you. The remainder of the sentence is in the third person, but answer C is a second-person reference. Therefore, it does not fit the sentence properly.

104. The detective *(A) <u>asked</u> the store for a list of all of the people *(B) <u>that had bought</u> milk *(C) <u>or yogurt</u> in the *(D) <u>past</u> week. *(E) <u>No Error</u>

The correct answer is B:) that had bought. The word "that" is used incorrectly in this sentence because "who" should always be used in reference to people.

105. *(A) <u>Erika worked</u> at *(B) <u>her computer</u> until *(C) <u>the report</u> was *(D) <u>finished</u>. *(E) <u>No Error</u>

The correct answer is E:) No Error. All of the verbs are in the same tense (past tense) and the case and references are all in agreement.

106. *(A) <u>I myself</u> am *(B) <u>responsible</u> for the errors *(C) <u>which</u> were present *(D) <u>in the document</u>. *(E) <u>No Error</u>

The correct answer is E:) No Error. This demonstrates correct usage of the reflexive reference of "myself."

107. The manager requested that *(A) <u>Neal and myself</u> supervise the *(B) <u>upcoming</u> company *(C) <u>retreat, and</u> provide the *(D) <u>refreshments afterwards</u>. *(E) <u>No Error</u>

The correct answer is A:) Neal and myself. This is an incorrect usage of the reflexive reference "myself." The correct reference would be "Neal and I."

108. After the *(A) <u>long boring day</u> at the *(B) <u>office, Kyle</u> was happy *(C) <u>to come home</u> and relax *(D) <u>in front of</u> the television. *(E) <u>No Error</u>

The correct answer is A:) long boring day. The day is described as both long and boring. Because both adjectives modify the noun day a comma is needed to separate them.

109. Alexandra *(A) <u>had become</u> an expert *(B) <u>at appeasing</u> customers after *(C) <u>7</u> years in the fast food *(D) <u>industry</u>. *(E) <u>No Error</u>

The correct answer is C:) 7 years. Numbers less than ten should always be in written form in a sentence. The sentence should read "after seven years."

110. *(A) <u>Nikki's</u> weight trainer *(B) <u>told her to</u> take a *(C) <u>ten-second</u> rest *(D) <u>after ten, twenty, and 30</u> reps. *(E) <u>No Error</u>

The correct answer is D:) after ten, twenty, and 30. The numbers are not parallel with each other. It should appear either with all numbers written, or all numbers is numeral form.

111. *(A) <u>Rodrigo chose</u> to *(B) <u>only</u> eat a burrito, rather *(C) <u>than</u> the tacos and en-chiladas that *(D) <u>he was also offered</u>. *(E) <u>No Error</u>

The correct answer is B:) only. Only is a misplaced modifier in this sentence. It should be placed before "a burrito" rather than "eat."

112. Cheng *(A) <u>had always been</u> fonder of *(B) <u>Science</u> *(C) <u>than</u> she had of *(D) <u>math</u>. *(E) <u>No Error</u>

The correct answer is B:) Science. In this sentence, science is referred to in a general manner; therefore, it does not need to be capitalized.

113. After *(A) <u>staying out</u> with friends until *(B) <u>two o'clock</u> in the morning, Sa-mantha *(C) <u>sleeped</u> until *(D) <u>late the next</u> afternoon. *(E) <u>No Error</u>

The correct answer is C:) sleeped. Sleep is an irregular verb, and its past-tense form is slept rather than sleeped.

114. The *(A) <u>company holds</u> an annual *(B) <u>breakfast</u>, with *(C) <u>pancakes, waffles, and scones</u>, *(D) <u>each year</u>. *(E) <u>No Error</u>

The correct answer is D:) each year. Because the sentence identifies the breakfast as an annual occurrence, it is redundant to also specify each year.

115. *(A) <u>Each</u> of the candidates *(B) <u>for the various</u> political parties *(C) <u>was</u> deter-mined that *(D) <u>they would be</u> the victor. *(E) <u>No Error</u>

The correct answer is D:) they would be. Although there are multiple candidates, the antecedent in this case is "each" which is a singular reference.

116. *(A) <u>Everyone</u> who reserved a seat *(B) <u>are</u> already here. *(C) <u>We are</u> just waiting for any *(D) <u>last-minute entrants</u>. *(E) <u>No Error</u>

The correct answer is B:) are. Everyone is a singular reference; therefore, the singular verb "is" should be used rather than the plural verb "are."

117. *(A) <u>Joan and Betty</u> are *(B) <u>really</u> excited for the upcoming concert; *(C) <u>their</u> going to see the *(D) <u>band together</u>. *(E) <u>No Error</u>

The correct answer is C:) their. This is the incorrect form of the word their to use in this sentence. Rather, the contraction "they're" should be used.

118. The *(A) <u>dog excitedly</u> pulled *(B) <u>it's</u> owner along *(C) <u>as it ran</u> after an *(D) <u>ice cream</u> truck. *(E) <u>No Error</u>

The correct answer is B:) it's. The possessive form of its does not contain an apostrophe. The apostrophe only appears in the contraction for it is.

119. *(A) <u>It's</u> quite a shame *(B) <u>that</u> the company *(C) <u>will be unable</u> to hold the annual *(D) <u>Christmas</u> party. *(E) <u>No Error</u>

The correct answer is E:) No Error. Christmas is correctly capitalized and the correct contraction "it's" is used in the sentence.

120. Courtney *(A) <u>was fond of</u> many exotic and unusual *(B) <u>foods: e.g.,</u> she *(C) <u>loved</u> alligator *(D) <u>burgers</u>. *(E) <u>No Error</u>

The correct answer is B:) foods: e.g. When "e.g." and "i.e." are used in a sentence, it is a semicolon, not a colon, which is used to set them apart.

121. The *(A) <u>manager made</u> many *(B) <u>errors in judgment</u> that *(C) <u>day; i.e.</u> he misplaced *(D) <u>all of</u> the money in the register. *(E) <u>No Error</u>

The correct answer is C:) day; i.e. To correctly use i.e., remember that it means "that is"; however, the sentence is introducing an example. This means that the correct term to use in this case is e.g.

122. Mrs. Richards *(A) <u>drove to</u> the store, *(B) <u>found the groceries</u> on her list, *(C) <u>put them in</u> her cart, *(D) <u>and will go</u> to the checkout. *(E) <u>No Error</u>

The correct answer is D:) and will go. This element does not follow the logical tense pattern that the rest of the sentence does. It should read "and went."

123. *(A) <u>After the jury</u> finally calmed *(B) <u>down, the judge told</u> the *(C) <u>prosecutor that he</u> could *(D) <u>precede questioning</u> the witness. *(E) <u>No Error</u>

The correct answer is D:) precede questioning. The word "precede" means to go before, and is used incorrectly in this context. Rather, the word proceed, or continue, should be used.

124. Samantha *(A) <u>fought</u> ardently with *(B) <u>her teacher</u> Ms. Anderson. *(C) <u>She</u> insisted that the assignment *(D) <u>had no errors</u>. *(E) <u>No Error</u>

The correct answer is C:) She. Both individuals identified in the first sentence are female. This makes the reference "she" unclear because it could refer to either of them.

125. Mrs. Swenson *(A) <u>told her son Albert</u> that *(B) <u>he had done</u> *(C) <u>really well</u> in his *(D) <u>soccer game</u>. *(E) <u>No Error</u>

The correct answer is E:) No Error. All of the verbs are in agreement in the sentence, and the word "well" is used correctly.

126. *(A) <u>Everyone</u> in the office *(B) <u>quickly</u> filled out *(C) <u>their</u> time card *(D) <u>at the end</u> of the day. *(E) <u>No Error</u>

The correct answer is C:) their. The subject "everyone" is singular. This means that the plural reference "their" is incorrect in this case.

127. *(A) <u>Your</u> going to *(B) <u>regret</u> it if *(C) <u>you</u> don't *(D) <u>go to college</u> one day. *(E) <u>No Error</u>

The correct answer is A:) Your. The correct word to use in this sentence is the contraction form of "you're," rather than the possessive form "your."

128. *(A) <u>I will</u> take *(B) <u>your</u> work *(C) <u>shift</u> *(D) <u>today, you</u> take my shift tomorrow. *(E) <u>No Error</u>

The correct answer is D:) today, you. A comma is not sufficient to join the two independent clauses. A coordinating conjunction, such as "if," is required.

129. *(A) <u>It is not correct</u> to join to *(B) <u>clauses without some</u> sort of *(C) <u>punctuation; and</u> often that *(D) <u>punctuation is</u> a comma or a semicolon. *(E) <u>No Error</u>

The correct answer is C:) punctuation; and. A semicolon should not be used to join to clauses when a semicolon is used.

130. When I *(A) <u>learned that</u> the environmental group *(B) <u>were protesting</u> the construction *(C) <u>project</u>, I *(D) <u>arranged</u> a meeting. *(E) <u>No Error</u>

The correct answer is B:) were protesting. The plural verb "were" is incorrect in this sentence because the subject is singular.

131. At the store yesterday, I *(A) <u>am going</u> to buy some *(B) <u>candy,</u> some *(C) <u>apples,</u> and some *(D) <u>macaroni and cheese</u>. *(E) <u>No Error</u>.

The correct answer is A:) am going. The introductory clause places the sentence is the past, so it is incorrect to use a progressive verb to describe the actions.

132. *(A) <u>Jonathan</u> *(B) <u>would not accept</u> the fact that Cindy *(C) <u>refused to go</u> to dinner *(D) <u>with him</u>. *(E) <u>No Error</u>

The correct answer is E:) No Error. All words are used correctly and all verbs and subjects are in agreement.

133. The *(A) <u>manager asked Joan</u> to find out *(B) <u>whether or not</u> the meeting *(C) <u>was scheduled</u> for the next *(D) <u>day?</u> *(E) <u>No Error</u>

The correct answer is D:) day? Although the word "whether" is used, it is not used as an interrogative in this case, and a question mark is not necessary.

134. *(A) <u>The supervisor</u> asked *(B) <u>Kim and I</u> to take an extra *(C) <u>shift</u> the *(D) <u>next day</u>. *(E) <u>No Error</u>

The correct answer is B:) Kim and I. The subjective "I" should not be used because the objective "me" is required in this context.

135. *(A) <u>Jon's and Matthew's</u> joint homework project *(B) <u>was going to be due</u> the next *(C) <u>week, and</u> they were hard at work *(D) <u>trying to finish</u> it. *(E) <u>No Error</u>

The correct answer is A:) Jon's and Mathew's. Because they are working on the project together, only Matthew's name is required to be in the possessive form. As written the sentence indicates that they each have their own projects, in which case it would not be "joint."

136. *(A) <u>The manager agreed</u> to change *(B) <u>me</u> shift to one *(C) <u>later in the day</u> so that I *(D) <u>could go to breakfast</u> with my grandmother. *(E) <u>No Error</u>

The correct answer is B:) me. The possessive "my" should be used instead of the objective "me."

137. *(A) <u>When my roommate</u> said that *(B) <u>she would not help</u> me clean the *(C) <u>bathroom, I</u> told her that I would do it *(D) <u>myself</u>. *(E) <u>No Error</u>

The correct answer is E:) No Error. This sentence makes correct use of the reflexive reference "myself."

138. The *(A) <u>security guard was</u> hard at work *(B) <u>trying to</u> determine *(C) <u>who's</u> fault the *(D) <u>burglary was</u>. *(E) <u>No Error</u>

The correct answer is C:) who's. The contraction for "who is" is incorrect in this context. Rather, the possessive "whose" should be used.

139. *(A) <u>Bryce had</u> not *(B) <u>been trained</u> for the *(C) <u>job, however,</u> he had a *(D) <u>natural talent</u> for it. *(E) <u>No Error</u>

The correct answer is C:) job, however. A semicolon is required in this context, rather than a comma.

140. Cynthia *(A) <u>would not</u> go to the store *(B) <u>alone, she</u> asked *(C) <u>her sister</u> to *(D) <u>come with</u> her. *(E) <u>No Error</u>

The correct answer is B:) alone, she. Because no conjunction is used, this is a comma splice.

141. I asked my sister not to wear *(A) <u>mine</u> clothes *(B) <u>without asking</u> me *(C) <u>first,</u> but she decided *(D) <u>not to listen</u> to me. *(E) <u>No Error</u>

The correct answer is A:) mine. Although mine is a possessive pronoun, the correct form to use in this context is "my."

142. The *(A) <u>CIO asked Louise</u> to be *(B) <u>sure</u> that all of the employees *(C) <u>receiving</u> a copy *(D) <u>of the recent</u> memo. *(E) <u>No Error</u>

The correct answer is C:) receiving. The progressive form of a verb cannot be used without a state of being verb with it (such as "are").

143. Sandra *(A) <u>wanted to be</u> certain *(B) <u>that her</u> son *(C) <u>was receiving</u> the best *(D) <u>treatment at the hospital</u>. *(E) <u>No Error</u>

The correct answer is E:) No Error. All of the verbs and subjects are in agreement.

144. The *(A) <u>document incorrectly</u> *(B) <u>stated that the</u> product *(C) <u>was "the</u> fastest on the *(D) <u>market".</u> *(E) <u>No Error</u>

The correct answer is D:) market". Periods should always appear inside quotation marks, not outside them.

145. *(A) <u>After Jenny broke</u> her leg, the *(B) <u>doctors told her</u> that she needed to remain *(C) <u>stationery,</u> and not go *(D) <u>anywhere for at least</u> two weeks. *(E) <u>No Error</u>

The correct answer is C:) stationery. The correct word to use in this context is stationary, or motionless.

146. The *(A) <u>manager's</u> all *(B) <u>gathered together</u> for a *(C) <u>meeting on the morning</u> of *(D) <u>the parade.</u> *(E) <u>No Error</u>

The correct answer is A:) manager's. The possessive form "manager's" is incorrect in this context. The plural "managers" is required instead.

147. *(A) <u>The teachers decided</u> that they would require *(B) <u>only</u> the students to take the final *(C) <u>exam, and</u> not the *(D) <u>midterm.</u> *(E) <u>No Error</u>

The correct answer is B:) only. This modifier is misplaced. It should be before the phrase "the final exam" which it is intended to modify, rather than "the students."

148. *(A) <u>The day after</u> the paper was *(B) <u>due, the student</u> told *(C) <u>her professor</u> that she *(D) <u>would write</u> the paper yesterday. *(E) <u>No Error</u>

The correct answer is D:) would write. This indicates a future occurrence, whereas the word "yesterday" indicates past. These two elements are not in agreement, so it must be incorrect.

149. Most *(A) <u>mountain peaks</u> in the *(B) <u>United States</u> can be *(C) <u>climbed during</u> a *(D) <u>weekend vacation.</u> *(E) <u>No Error</u>

The correct answer is E:) No Error. The correct plurals are used, and all verbs and subjects are in agreement.

150. The employees *(A) <u>that</u> were newly hired *(B) <u>were required to attend</u> four days of *(C) <u>rigorous training</u> before their first shift *(D) <u>was scheduled.</u> *(E) <u>No Error</u>

The correct answer is A:) that. People, such as the employees, should be referred to as "who."

SECTION 1 ANSWER KEY

1. D	42. B	83. C	124. C
2. C	43. A	84. A	125. E
3. A	44. A	85. B	126. C
4. C	45. D	86. A	127. A
5. D	46. C	87. D	128. D
6. D	47. B	88. B	129. C
7. D	48. C	89. E	130. B
8. A	49. E	90. C	131. A
9. B	50. D	91. B	132. E
10. C	51. D	92. A	133. D
11. E	52. C	93. E	134. B
12. A	53. D	94. D	135. A
13. D	54. E	95. D	136. B
14. C	55. D	96. B	137. E
15. B	56. C	97. C	138. C
16. D	57. A	98. A	139. C
17. B	58. B	99. B	140. B
18. C	59. C	100. D	141. A
19. E	60. E	101. A	142. C
20. D	61. C	102. D	143. E
21. A	62. C	103. C	144. D
22. A	63. A	104. B	145. C
23. E	64. B	105. E	146. A
24. C	65. D	106. E	147. B
25. B	66. D	107. A	148. D
26. A	67. B	108. A	149. E
27. C	68. D	109. C	150. A
28. D	69. C	110. D	
29. D	70. E	111. B	
30. E	71. C	112. B	
31. A	72. A	113. C	
32. B	73. A	114. D	
33. C	74. B	115. D	
34. B	75. D	116. B	
35. A	76. B	117. C	
36. D	77. A	118. B	
37. C	78. D	119. E	
38. C	79. E	120. B	
39. E	80. C	121. C	
40. B	81. D	122. D	
41. C	82. D	123. D	

Section 2: Improving Sentences

FIXING INCORRECT SENTENCE BOUNDARIES

Once you understand the rules for sentence boundaries and basic punctuation, you will have no trouble recognizing correct sentences. Correct sentences:

1. Have a subject, verb, and sense of completeness in each sentence.

2. Should be parallel in structure.

3. Should have modifying clauses next to the noun they describe.

4. Must use commas with conjunctions when combining two independent clauses.

5. Use semicolons only between two independent phrases.

6. May use semicolons to connect two related sentences.

7. May use semicolons with a conjunctive adverb to illustrate the connection between two sentences.

Remember: Length does NOT determine whether a sentence is correct. Some writers, Faulkner, Fitzgerald, and Poe, to name just a few, wrote perfectly correct sentences of a hundred words or more. A one-word sentence, if it's a direct command, like, "Wait!" can also be a correct sentence. Don't fall into the trap of believing that just because it's a long sentence, it must be a run-on. Study the punctuation and the meaning, and determine whether the essential rules have been followed.

HOW TO FIX A COMMA SPLICE:

1. Put a period in between the two sentences:

    WRONG: I can't go to school today, I will go tomorrow.
    CORRECT: I can't go to school today. I will go tomorrow.

2. Use a comma with one of the coordinating conjunctions (for, and, nor, but, or, yet, so). Think of these conjunctions as a kind of glue. You can't have two sentences combined without them.

    WRONG: I can't go to school today, I will go tomorrow.
    CORRECT: I can't go to school today, so I will go tomorrow.
    CORRECT: I can't go to school today, but I will go tomorrow.

TIP: Memorize the seven coordinating conjunctions. Remember that the word "then" is NOT a conjunction, and so you must add in one of these words when it is used.

3. Use a semicolon to attach two sentences together. A semicolon is used to connect two sentences that are closely related in meaning. In general, use a semicolon in the same place as you would a period.

    WRONG: The dog just ran into the street, he was running when he was hit by a car.
    CORRECT: The dog just ran into the street; he was running when he was hit by a car.

4. Use a semicolon to attach two sentences together with a word known as a conjunctive adverb. Conjunctive adverbs are words like however, therefore, subsequently, consequently, moreover, also, certainly, in addition, and otherwise.

    WRONG: I can't go to school today, I will go tomorrow.
    CORRECT: I can't go to school today; however, I will go tomorrow.

HOW TO FIX A RUN-ON SENTENCE:

1. The easiest way to fix a run-on sentence is to break it up into two sentences. You may also use some of the same repair strategies that you use for comma splices.

    WRONG: Love means many different things to many people it's hard to give a distinct definition of it.
    CORRECT: Love means many different things to many people. It's hard to give a distinct definition of it.

2. Utilize a semicolon in between the two independent clauses.

    WRONG: Love means many different things to many people it's hard to give a distinct definition of it.
    CORRECT: Love means many different things to many people; it's hard to give a distinct definition of it.

3. Utilize a semicolon AND a conjunctive adverb between the two independent clauses.

   WRONG: Love means many different things to many people it's hard to give a distinct definition of it.

   CORRECT: Love means many different things to many people; therefore, it's hard to give a distinct definition of it.

4. Insert a comma and a conjunction between the two word groups.

   WRONG: Love means many different things to many people it's hard to give a distinct definition of it.

   CORRECT: Love means many different things to many people, and it's hard to give a distinct definition of it.

5. Make one of the phrases a DEPENDENT clause so that it has to rely on the other clause to make it a complete sentence.

   WRONG: Love means many different things to many people it's hard to give a distinct definition of it.

   CORRECT: Since love means many different things to many people, it's hard to give a distinct definition of it.

HOW TO FIX A SENTENCE FRAGMENT:

1. Combine the dependent clause with another independent clause.

   WRONG: I know he didn't commit the crime. Because he was at the movies.

   CORRECT: I know he didn't commit the crime because he was at the movies.

2. Remember that a gerund (an "-ing" verb) is not a verb unless it has one of the helping verbs with it.

TIP: Memorize the helping verbs: is, am, are, was, were, be, being, been, has, have, had, do, does, did, can, could, shall, should, will, would, may, might, must.

   WRONG: The boy swimming in the ocean.

   CORRECT: The boy was swimming in the ocean.

3. Pay close attention to the first word of the sentence. Transitional words often cause students to write a fragment. Again, this error is caused by relying on the previous sentence for the meaning instead of paying attention to each of the word groups. Correct it by combining it with a complete sentence.

WRONG: She had lots of health problems. Like an irregular heartbeat and migraine headaches.

CORRECT: She had lots of health problems like an irregular heartbeat and migraine headaches.

CORRECT: She had lots of health problems. Two of the most chronic problems were an irregular heartbeat and migraine headaches.

PUNCTUATION

1. Commas
   Probably the cause of more errors than other punctuation, don't fear the common comma. All you need is some basic guidelines to whip this little device into shape.
   Forget any teacher who told you to put a comma in wherever you pause. That's bad advice! Commas are used for specific reasons:

   a. To hold together two independent clauses WITH a conjunction.
   b. To set off any introductory word, dependent phrase, or descriptive clause that comes at the beginning of a sentence.
   c. To separate non-essential information from the rest of the sentence.
   d. To separate items in a series.
   e. To set off transitional expressions or parenthetical information.
   f. To set off direct addresses, interjections, and tag questions.
   g. To set off quotations.
   h. To set off parts of addresses, titles, numbers, and dates.

2. Semicolons
   a. To link two closely-related independent clauses together.
   b. To link two closely-related independent clauses together with a conjunctive adverb.
   c. To separate items in a series containing other punctuation to clarify the meaning and make the sentence easier to read.

3. Question marks
   a. Put at the end of a sentence that asks a question.
   b. Use at the end of direct questions, not after indirect questions which often include the word "whether," or "that." (He asked whether I was going to the show. / She asked that I not tell anyone.)

4. Apostrophes
    a. Used in contractions to show where an omission occurs: can't = cannot / doesn't = does not.
    b. Used to show possession. An apostrophe + s, indicates that the item belongs to someone: The girl's purse was on the floor of the car.
       The bus's wheels were spinning in the mud.
       The men's fitness center was always crowded.
    c. Used by itself or with an –s to show possession of a singular word that ends in –s.
       Charles' favorite vehicle was an old Chevrolet Nova that he had rebuilt.
       Charles's favorite vehicle was an old Chevrolet Nova that he had rebuilt.
       (Either of the above is correct.)
    d. Used by itself to show possession of a plural word that ends in an –s.
       The three bridesmaids' dresses hung on the back of the door.

5. Quotation Marks
    a. Indicate direct, verbatim quotes.
    b. Single quotation marks are placed around a quote inside a quote.
    c. Placed around titles of short works of poems, essays, songs, articles, and individual episodes of television or radio programs.
    d. Put around definitions.
       TIP: Commas and periods are always placed inside quotation marks. Semicolons and colons are placed outside of quotation marks. Question marks and exclamation marks are placed inside quotes if they apply to the quotation itself; outside if the marks apply to the entire sentence.

6. Colons
    a. Introduce an example, appositive, or an explanation.
    b. Introduce a series, a quotation, or a list if the introductory material is a complete sentence:
       The wife made a list of all the necessary ingredients for bread pudding and directed her husband to pick them all up: bread, sugar, milk, raisins, and eggs.
    c. Separate ratios, salutations on formal letters, Biblical references, and elements of time.

7. Ellipsis
    a. Use an ellipsis to indicate where words have been omitted from a quoted passage.

8. Hyphens
   a. Used when a prefix ends with the same letter that the main word begins in
   b. Used to clarify the meaning of a word so it is not mistaken for another
   c. The prefix is "self"
   d. The main word is a proper noun
   e. Used when two adjectives, preceding a noun, act jointly (only when preceding a noun)

SYNTAX

Don't let the word scare you. "Syntax" is a fancy term that simply means how words are put together. Your understanding of syntax is encapsulated in your brain from the time you learned how to talk, but a few small "polishing points" could improve your writing.

Parallelism: Think of parallel bars or parallel lines. Both are images that look just like each other. That's exactly what it means in language as well. Whenever you have three items in a series, they must all be alike, and NOT like the following sentence where the third verb doesn't match the first two.

> "The young girl skipped, laughed, and was singing a limerick as she went down the street."

Since parallelism means that all the items in a series look the same, the third verb must be put into the simple past tense.

> "The young girl skipped, laughed, and sang a limerick as she went down the street."

Another type of parallelism is comparing two items for emphasis. One of the most famous examples is Patrick Henry's line, "Give me liberty, or give me death." If he had uttered, "Give me liberty or death," the statement would never have gone down in history as a great moment of oratory. The use of parallel structure made it work.

Coordination: Coordination is the term that refers to how you connect ideas together. When you connect two sentences with a comma and one of the seven conjunctions (for, and, nor, but, or, yet, so), then you are basically giving each of the ideas equal importance.

> "The house was huge, and it was expensive."

Subordination: Subordination is a term similar to coordination because it refers to how you put ideas together, but instead of making the ideas equal in importance, subordination makes one idea "subordinate" to the other. The idea with more weight is placed in the independent clause. The less important idea is then placed in a dependent clause.

"Even though the ring didn't cost much, it was my most treasured possession."

<u>Modifiers</u>: A "modifier" is simply a descriptive phrase or word. A "misplaced modifier" happens when a descriptive phrase is placed next to a noun, but it's not the noun it's supposed to describe.

As a young girl, Bobby walked me to school.

Notice that the descriptive phrase is placed next to the noun Bobby. Now, wouldn't Bobby be horrified to think that he was once a young girl?

The simplest cure for a misplaced modifier is to make sure that the descriptive phrase is placed nearest the noun which it modifies.

As a young girl, I often found Bobby walking me to school OR
As a young man, Bobby often walked me to school.

IDIOM

Foreign speakers often have trouble with idioms, phrases that are difficult to comprehend because they don't have a literal meaning. Phrases like, "it's a piece of cake," "he bought the farm," and "raining cats and dogs." If English is your second language, you might want to invest in a dictionary of idioms and colloquial sayings, and above all, listen to expressions used in daily conversation so that you can begin to understand the "figurative" language that is so often a part of life.

One idiomatic phrase that that's difficult to distinguish is the use of prepositions. "In" and "on" are particularly hard.

The word "in" is typically used when referring to something that occurs in a particular time or space:

The plane arrived in Florida after a storm delay.

The word "on" is typically used with dates and street names.

He was born on May 11, 1958.
He was lost on First Avenue.

ACTIVE VOICE

The preferred kind of sentence in the English language, it simply means that the subject of the sentence is doing the action.

"The cat chased the mouse" is an active sentence. The cat is performing the action, "chased."

The same sentence becomes passive, however, if the subject is being acted upon instead of performing the action: "The mouse was chased by the cat."

For the vast majority of the time, sentences should be written in the active voice.

MODIFIERS

Modifiers (adjectives and adverbs) are an integral and common part of the English language. In order for writing to make sense it is important that they are used correctly. A few guidelines to ensure that modifiers are used correctly are presented below.

1. Move modifying phrases next to the phrases that they are intended to modify.

   WRONG: Sam asked her to dance **timidly**. *Timidly should be near Sam, not dance.*
   CORRECT: Sam **timidly** asked her to dance.

   WRONG: I'm renting the boat to the family **with the broken oar**.
   CORRECT: I'm renting the boat **with a broken oar** to the family.

2. Specifically with the modifying word "only" be sure that it is near the correct phrase.

   WRONG: This summer I am **only** going to Chicago, and to no other places. *"Only" is meant to describe the number of places, not that the speaker is "only going."*
   CORRECT: This summer I am going **only** to Chicago, and to no other places.

3. Make sure introductory phrases describe the subject of the following clause.

   WRONG: Growing five feet in one summer, Martha was proud of her sunflower crop. *The introductory phrase does not describe Martha, but the sunflower crop.*
   CORRECT: Martha was proud of her sunflower crop because it grew five feet in one summer.
   CORRECT: Because it grew five feet in one summer, Martha was proud of her sunflower crop.

NUMBERS

There are really only three basic rules to remember when working with numbers.

1. Spell out any numbers ten or lower (one, two, three, etc.)
2. Use numerals for any numbers greater than ten (11, 35, 20, etc.)
3. For very large numbers, use a combination of words and numbers (25 million, 10 thousand, etc.)

Of course, there are some exceptions to these generalities as well.

1. Always spell out a word at a beginning of a sentence (One day…, Thirty days later…, etc.)
2. Always use numerals for percentages (9 percent, 4 percent, 35 percent, etc.)
3. If numbers are used in a list, keep the same formatting (4 cars, 3 trucks, and 20 jeeps – all are in numerals because "20" is in numerals).

Sample Questions – Test Yourself

Choose the answer choice that best improves or corrects the underlined portion of the sentence.

1. If a nation values anything more than freedom, it will lose its freedom; <u>and the irony of it is that if it is comfort or money that it values more, it will lose that too</u>.
   – W. Somerset Maugham

   A) and the irony of it is that if it is comfort or money that it values more, it will lose that too
   B) and the irony of it is that whether it is comfort or whether it is money that it values most, it will lose that too
   C) and the irony of it is that if it is comfort or money that it values more; it will lose that too
   D) and the irony of it is that if it is comfort or money that it values more, it will lose those too
   E) and the irony of it is that if it is comfort or money that it values more, it will lose that too

2. Nothing in the world can take the place of persistence. <u>Talent will not, nothing is more common than unsuccessful men with talent. Genius will not, unrewarded genius is almost a proverb. Education will not, the world is full of educated derelicts.</u> Persistence and determination are omnipotent.

   A) Talent will not, nothing is more common than unsuccessful men with talent. Genius will not, unrewarded genius is almost a proverb. Education will not, the world is full of educated derelicts.
   B) Talent will not; nothing is more common than unsuccessful men with talent. Genius will not; unrewarded genius is almost a proverb. Education will not; the world is full of educated derelicts.
   C) Talent will never do it: nothing is more common than unsuccessful men with talent. Genius will not do it; unrewarded genius is almost a proverb. Education can't do it; the world is full of educated derelicts.
   D) Talent will not; nothing is more common than unsuccessful men with talent. Genius will not; unrewarded genius is almost a proverb. An education will not; the world is full of educated derelicts.
   E) Talent isn't; nothing is more common than unsuccessful men with talent. Genius won't; unrewarded genius is almost a proverb. An education doesn't; the world is full of educated derelicts.

3. <u>When I knew I was going to live this long, I'd have taken better care of myself.</u> – Mickey Mantle

   A) When I knew I was going to live this long; I'd have taken better care of myself.
   B) If I knew I was going to live this long; I'd have taken better care of myself.
   C) If I knew I was going to live this long, I'd have taken better care of myself.
   D) If I knew I was going to live this long, I will have take better care of myself.
   E) Since I knew I was going to live this long, I took better care of myself.

4. I can't imagine that <u>he is the killer he was on vacation</u> at the time of the murder.

   A) he is the killer he was on vacation
   B) he would be the killer he would have gone on vacation
   C) he is the killer he is on vacation
   D) he had been the killer; he was on vacation
   E) he is the killer. He was on vacation

5. <u>I going to the store later today.</u>

   A) I going to the store later today
   B) Later today, I would have been going to the store
   C) I was going to be going to the store later today
   D) I am going to the store later today
   E) Going to the store, I am later today

6. <u>The four and six-inch sandwiches</u> were meant to be served at the luncheon.

   A) The four and six-inch sandwiches
   B) The four and six-inch sandwich's
   C) The four- and six-inch sandwiches
   D) The four- and six-inch sandwich's
   E) The four and six inch sandwiches

7. <u>Jared offered his counsel</u> to the applicant.

   A) Jared was going to have offered his council
   B) Offering his, Jared counseled
   C) Jared offered his council
   D) Jared was wanting to have answered his counsel
   E) Jared offered his counsel

8. He <u>would have liked to have considered</u> the matter further.

    A) would have liked to have considered
    B) would have liked to consider
    C) liked to would have considered
    D) wanted to have liked considering
    E) was considering liking

9. Although Sarah <u>wanted only the red box</u>, she had to buy the blue box and the green box as well.

    A) wanted only the red box
    B) only wanted the red box
    C) wanted the only red box
    D) wanted the red only box
    E) was wanting only the red boxes

10. <u>Spinning in circles, Sadie was mystified by the top</u>.

    A) Spinning in circles, Sadie was mystified by the top
    B) Spun in circles, Sadie was mystified by the top
    C) Circling and spinning the Sadie was mystified by the top
    D) Sadie was mystified by the top because it was spinning in circles
    E) After having spun in circles, Sadie found the top mystifying

SAMPLE QUESTION KEY – TEST YOURSELF

1. B
2. B
3. C
4. E
5. D
6. C
7. E
8. B
9. A
10. D

SECTION 2: IMPROVING SENTENCES QUESTIONS

Choose the answer choice that best improves or corrects the underlined portion of the sentence.

1. The group that went to the semifinals was the group which came in first place in the quarterfinals.

   A) The group that went to
   B) The group which went to
   C) The group who went
   D) The group which will go
   E) The groups that went

2. Even though the car that Melissa wanted to buy cost $20,000, she only decided to borrow $5,000.

   A) she only decided to borrow $5,000
   B) she chose to borrowed $5,000 only
   C) only she decided to borrow $5,000
   D) she decided only to borrow $5,000
   E) she decided to borrow only $5,000

3. Sam's parents had always told him that they loved him very much.

   A) Sam's parents had always
   B) Sam's parent's had always
   C) Sams parent's always had
   D) Sam's parent's always had
   E) Always, Sam's parents had

4. Ashley was embarrassed how the news spread that she had been in a car wreck.

   A) was embarrassed how the news spread
   B) was embarrassed when the news began to spread
   C) was embarrassed for the news spreading
   D) was embarrassing that the news spread
   E) was embarrassed that the news had begun to start spreading

5. After migrating to America in 1950, <u>in San Francisco is where my grandparents opened their donut shop</u>.

    A) in San Francisco is where my grandparents opened their donut shop
    B) a donut shop was opened in San Francisco by my grandparents
    C) San Francisco is where my grandparents opened their own donut shop, and began selling the greatest donuts in all of the Western United States
    D) my grandparents opened a donut shop in San Francisco
    E) in San Francisco my grandparents opened a donut shop

6. Aaron told his mom the swing set on the playground <u>broke</u> for many years.

    A) broke
    B) had broken
    C) had been broke
    D) would broke
    E) had been broken

7. She signaled to change lanes, <u>after she moved into the left lane</u>.

    A) after she moved into the left lane
    B) and then she moved into the left lane
    C) then she after turned into the left lane
    D) because she then wanted to turn into the left lane
    E) for she wanted to stay in her same lane after

8. I asked the teacher if <u>I and Jim</u> could be the first group to give a report.

    A) I and Jim
    B) Jim and me
    C) Jim and I
    D) me and Jim
    E) Jim and myself

9. When the man won the presidential election, <u>people celebrated by doing fireworks</u>.

    A) people celebrated by doing fireworks
    B) people doing fireworks celebrated
    C) people celebrated doing fireworks
    D) celebrating, people did fireworks
    E) people did fireworks celebrating

10. The car stopped working because <u>it's</u> engine was overheated.

    A) it's
    B) it is
    C) that's
    D) its
    E) his

11. <u>Throwing a tantrum, the mother told her son to</u> do his chores.

    A) Throwing a tantrum, the mother told her son to
    B) The mother throwing a tantrum told her son to
    C) The son told his mother, who was throwing a tantrum, to
    D) The mother told her tantrum-throwing children to
    E) The mother told her son, who was throwing a tantrum, to

12. The doctor told the patient that he was <u>going to both administer anesthetic and stitch the cut</u>.

    A) going to both administer anesthetic and stitch the cut
    B) going both to administer anesthetic and stick the cut
    C) both administering anesthetic and then going to stitch the cut
    D) going to both administer and stitch anesthetic and the cut
    E) both going to administer anesthetic and then stitch the cut

13. Amber told the car salesman that the <u>car that was green</u> was her favorite.

    A) car that was green
    B) car who was green
    C) car, that was green,
    D) car, who was green,
    E) green, that was a car,

14. If the food is too cold for the baby, <u>put it in the oven for a minute</u>.

    A) put it in the oven for a minute
    B) put the food in the oven for a minute
    C) put the oven in it for a minute
    D) put the baby in the oven for a minute
    E) put the food for a minute in the oven

15. <u>When she</u> realized the car would break down, then she would have changed the oil before going on the road trip.

    A) When she
    B) After she
    C) If she had
    D) If she
    E) Before

16. The money that Martha spent was less than <u>it which her children spent</u>.

    A) it which her children spent
    B) the money, which her children spent
    C) that which her children spent
    D) what monies her children spent
    E) her children was spending

17. The Constitution is <u>newer than it but just as important as the Declaration of Independence</u>.

    A) newer than it but just as important as the Declaration of Independence
    B) just as new as the Declaration of Independence but is important
    C) newer than the Declaration of Independence: but it is important
    D) newer and more important than the Declaration of Independence
    E) newer than, but just as important as, the Declaration of Independence

18. A common theme of horror stories, a full moon <u>has been blamed for the howling of dogs, the thirst of vampires, the advent of lunacy, and increasing births</u>.

    A) has been blamed for the howling of dogs, the thirst of vampires, the advent of lunacy, and increasing births
    B) has been blamed for the howling of dogs, the thirst of vampires, the advent of lunacy, and the increase of births
    C) has been blamed for; howling dogs, thirsting vampires, beginning lunacy, increasing births
    D) was blaming for the howling of dogs, the thirst of vampires, the advent of lunacy, and increasing births
    E) had been blamed that dogs howl, vampires thirst, the advent of lunacy, and that births increase

19. <u>It was a shame that</u> Jenny could not make it to the party.

    A) It was a shame that
    B) That was a shame it that
    C) It was that a shame when
    D) When was a shame if
    E) That was a shame that

20. I had always been taught <u>that two plus two was four</u>.

    A) that two plus two was four
    B) it that two plus two was four
    C) that two plus two is four
    D) two plus two was equal to four
    E) it; two plus two was four

21. The manager <u>hadn't went to lock up the vault yet</u> when the robber entered the bank.

    A) hadn't went to lock up the vault yet
    B) hadn't yet went to lock up the vault
    C) to lock up the vault hadn't yet gone
    D) hadn't yet gone to lock up the vault
    E) hadn't gone to lock up the vault yet

22. Jonah never received his letter because the post office could not read that <u>it was him whom that was addressed to</u>.

    A) it was him whom that was addressed to
    B) it was him to whom it was addressed
    C) it was him that it was addressed to
    D) it was he who it was addressed to
    E) it was he who that was addressed to

23. <u>Neither the manager or the supervisor was</u> aware that Henry was not coming into work that day.

    A) Neither the manager or the supervisor was
    B) Neither the manager nor the supervisor was
    C) Either the manager nor the super were
    D) Both the manager or the supervisor was
    E) Neither the manager or the supervisor were

24. <u>All of the candy are being saved</u> for next Halloween.

   A) All of the candy are being saved
   B) All of the candies is being saved
   C) All of the candy are saving
   D) All of the candy was saving
   E) All of the candy is being saved

25. <u>The memo was typed by the secretary, and then it was sent out</u> to be distributed throughout the office.

   A) The memo was typed by the secretary, and then it was sent out
   B) The secretary was typing the memo, later she sent it out
   C) The secretary typed the memo and sent it out
   D) The secretary had been typing the memo and then sending it out
   E) The memo typed by the secretary, and was sent out

26. Because he was late to class <u>was the reason that Jonathan was embarrassed to</u> meet the teacher.

   A) was the reason that Jonathan was embarrassed to
   B) ; Jonathan had to be embarrassed for that reason to
   C) was to Jonathan the reason to be embarrassed to
   D) embarrassed was how Jonathan had reason to
   E) Jonathan was embarrassed to

27. <u>I wanted to have gone</u> to the store, but I didn't have enough time.

   A) I wanted to have gone
   B) I wanted to go
   C) I wished to have gone
   D) I want to have gone
   E) I want to have went

28. <u>If I was to go to the store</u>, I would want to buy chocolate ice cream.

   A) If I was to go to the store
   B) Was I to go to the store
   C) If I were to go to the store
   D) Then I went to the store
   E) Was I going to the store

29. Samantha <u>was sure happy that she was invited</u> to go to the seminar.

    A) was sure happy that she was invited
    B) was sure happy that she were invited
    C) surely was happy to be invited
    D) was surely happy that she was invited
    E) was invited and surely happy

30. <u>The manager complemented Jane on</u> her excellent work drafting the memos and filing the paperwork.

    A) The manager complemented Jane on
    B) The manager complimented Jane in
    C) The manager complemented Jane in
    D) Jane was complimented by the manager on
    E) The manager complimented Jane on

31. The managers <u>were going not only to Chicago, but also to Pittsburg</u> to check on progress in their offices.

    A) were going not only to Chicago, but also to Pittsburg
    B) was going to Chicago not only, but to Pittsburg also
    C) were going to both Chicago, but also to Pittsburg
    D) were also to Chicago, not only to Pittsburg
    E) was not going only to Chicago, but going also to Pittsburg

32. Generally the dogs <u>were taken to the kennel Monday mornings usually</u>.

    A) were taken to the kennel Monday mornings usually
    B) were taken to the kennel Monday mornings
    C) were usually taken Monday mornings to the kennel
    D) were taked to the kennels Monday morning
    E) were took to the kennel Monday mornings usually

33. Beagles and Labradors <u>is two different breeds of dogs</u>.

    A) is two different breeds of dogs
    B) is dogs of two different breeds
    C) are two different breeds of dogs
    D) breed two different types of dogs
    E) are types of dogs of two different breeds

34. <u>Each of the teachers are required to</u> return graded papers to students within a week.

    A) Each of the teachers are required to
    B) The teachers is each required to
    C) The teachers each are required to
    D) Each teachers are required to
    E) Each of the teachers is required to

35. The children could not go to the park that day <u>because it was raining cats and dogs</u>.

    A) because it was raining cats and dogs
    B) because cats and dogs were falling from the sky
    C) because it was raining heavily
    D) because there were cats and dogs raining
    E) because there were lots of cats of dogs and it was raining

36. The supervisor was more <u>impressed by the second applicant than the first</u>.

    A) impressed by the second applicant than the first
    B) impressed with the second applicant then the first applicant
    C) impressed by the second applicant than more than the first
    D) impressed by the second applicant than by the first applicant
    E) pleased by the first applicant than expressed by the second applicant

37. <u>Everything in the room were</u> used for decorating cakes.

    A) Everything in the room were
    B) Everything in the room was
    C) Was everything in the room
    D) In the room, everything were
    E) Everything, in the room, were

38. Jennifer was angry with her mother; <u>she told her that the job was not a good idea</u>.

    A) she told her that the job was not a good idea
    B) her told she that the job was not a good idea
    C) she had told her that the job was not a good idea
    D) it was not a good idea, she had told her, to take the job
    E) her mother had told her that the job was not a good idea

39. The oil tycoon <u>had spent the last 30 years and built</u> his business.

    A) had spent the last 30 years and built
    B) spent the last 30 years and built
    C) had spent the last 30 years building
    D) having spent the last 30 years building
    E) spending his last 30 years building

40. <u>Dave and me went</u> to the store and bought three potatoes for the soup.

    A) Dave and me went
    B) Me and Dave went
    C) Dave and I had went
    D) I and Dave went
    E) Dave and I went

41. <u>The Smith's and the Wilson's cars</u> both had to be taken to the shop to be fixed.

    A) The Smith's and the Wilson's cars
    B) The Smith and the Wilson's cars
    C) The Smith's and the Wilson car's
    D) The Smith's and the Wilson's cars'
    E) The Smith and the Wilson car's

42. The receptionist <u>finished the long detailed memo</u> just before her shift ended.

    A) finished the long detailed memo
    B) finished the long, detailed memo
    C) finished the long-detailed memo
    D) finished typing the long, and detailed memo
    E) finish the detailed memo which was very long

43. At my request, my mother <u>took Christine and me</u> to the store to buy soup.

    A) took Christine and me
    B) taked Christine and me
    C) took me and Christine
    D) took Christine and I
    E) took I and Christine

44. The manager announced to all of the employees that a new policy would require that they all have <u>weekly interviews with he</u>.

    A) weekly interviews with he
    B) an interview each week with he
    C) meet with him weekly each week for an interview
    D) weekly interviews with him
    E) weekly interviews with him each week

45. Neither of the candidates, after traveling to many different states and talking to many different people, <u>were sure that they would win the election</u>.

    A) were sure that they would win the election
    B) were sure that he would win the election
    C) was sure that they would win the election
    D) had surety that he would be the winner of the upcoming national election
    E) was sure that he would win the election

46. After returning from the store, <u>she recalled that she was out of toilet paper</u>.

    A) she recalled that she was out of toilet paper
    B) she recalled it that she was out of toilet paper
    C) she recalled the toilet paper that she was out of
    D) it was recalled by her that she was out of toilet paper
    E) she recalled that her was out of toilet paper

47. <u>The officer asked who's</u> red car was parked in the third stall from the end.

    A) The officer asked who's
    B) The officer asked whos
    C) The officer asked whose
    D) The officer asked whom's
    E) The officer asked which

48. The company put <u>their carefully-calculated strategy</u> into effect.

    A) their carefully-calculated strategy
    B) the carefully-calculated strategy
    C) it's carefully calculated strategy
    D) its carefully-calculated strategy
    E) its carefully calculated strategy

49. The course required that each student possess a <u>pencil and paper, a desk and chair and a computer and mouse</u>.

    A) pencil and paper, a desk and chair and a computer and mouse
    B) pencil and paper, a desk and chair, and a computer and mouse
    C) pencils, papers, desks, chairs, computers, mice.
    D) pencil, and paper, a desk, and chair, and a computer, and mouse
    E) pencils and papers, desks and chairs, computers and mice

50. As a highly skilled detective, <u>the captain was sure that Jon would be an excellent guest speaker at the conference</u>.

    A) the captain was sure that Jon would be an excellent guest speaker at the conference
    B) the captain, Jon felt, would make an excellent speaker at the conference
    C) the captain determined that Jon would be an excellent speaker
    D) Jon would make an excellent guest speaker at the conference
    E) Jon, the captain were sure, would be an excellent guest speaker at the conference

51. GM had started production of <u>the cars in 1995 it was fully aware</u> of the brake problems.

    A) the cars in 1995 it was fully aware
    B) the cars in 1995; it was fully aware
    C) the cars in 1995, it was fully aware
    D) the cars in 1995: it was fully aware
    E) the cars in 1995. Being fully aware

52. Henry James wrote a story called *The Turn of the Screw* <u>in fact the story has nothing</u> to do with carpentry.

    A) Screw in fact the story has nothing
    B) Screw; however, the story has nothing
    C) Screw but the story has nothing
    D) Screw still the story has nothing
    E) Screw, although the story has nothing

53. Eighteen people have contracted the plague in New Mexico <u>this year as a matter of fact,</u> there are more cases than in any state since 1925.

    A) this year as a matter of fact
    B) this year and as a matter of fact
    C) this year; as a matter of fact
    D) this year, as a matter of fact
    E) this year. As a matter of fact

54. Most <u>mountain peaks in the</u> United States can be climbed during a weekend vacation.

    A) mountain peaks in the
    B) mountains peaks in the
    C) mountain peak's in the
    D) mountain peaks' in the
    E) mountains' peak in the

55. Until the cause of the <u>disease is found people will</u> continue to die.

    A) disease is found people will
    B) disease is found: people will
    C) disease is found; people will
    D) disease is found, people will
    E) disease is found. People will

56. Dragonflies <u>have large eyes who look like</u> jewels.

    A) have large eyes who look like
    B) have large eyes rather look like
    C) have large eyes that look like
    D) have large eyes which look like
    E) have large eyes; which look like

57. Jody said that the drawing <u>was she's.</u>

    A) was she's
    B) was hers
    C) is she's
    D) is hers
    E) was herselfs

58. From the airplane, the river seemed languid, serene, and tranquilly flowed toward the sea.

    A) From the airplane, the river seemed languid, serene, and tranquilly flowed toward the sea.
    B) From the airplane, the river seemed languid, serene, and tranquil as it flowing toward the sea.
    C) From the airplane, the river seemed languid, serene, and tranquilly flowing toward the sea.
    D) From the airplane, the river seemed languid, serene and flowed tranquilly toward the sea.
    E) The river seemed languid, serene, tranquilly flowing toward the sea and could be seen from the airplane.

59. They associate pain to being a hyper-consumer and pleasure to being frugal.

    A) pain to being a hyper-consumer and pleasure to being frugal
    B) pain with being a hyper-consumer and pleasure to being frugal
    C) pain to being a hyper-consumer and pleasure with being frugal
    D) pain with being a hyper-consumer and pleasure with being frugal
    E) pain because being a hyper-consumer and pleasure to being frugal

60. The reason I don't approve of research projects conducted in schools is because we must protect our liberties.

    A) is because we must protect our liberties
    B) ; however, we must protect our liberties
    C) is that we must protect our liberties
    D) is that, we must protect our liberties
    E) is for we must protect our liberties

61. All the girls were looked on as a sister in the camp.

    A) as a sister in the camp
    B) as sisters in the camp
    C) like a sister in the camp
    D) being a sister in the camp
    E) to be a sister in the camp

62. The legs of <u>the chair will be replace</u> because they are worn.

    A) the chair will be replace
    B) the chairs will have been replaced
    C) the chairs will be replaced
    D) the chairs can be replace
    E) the chairs be replaced

63. They believed that their son had died <u>when the ship sunk</u>.

    A) when the ship sunk
    B) after the ship sunk
    C) during the ship's sunk
    D) through the ship's sank
    E) when the ship sank

64. The supervisor <u>has spoken to the men</u> about locking the door at night.

    A) has spoken to the men
    B) have spoken to the men
    C) will spoken to the men
    D) has speaked to the men
    E) mist spoken to the men

65. <u>Janie's professor told her that she should find a better place to study. She needed to spend less time visiting with her friends, and ought to attend class more frequently.</u>

    A) Janie's professor told her that she should find a better place to study. She needed to spend less time visiting with her friends, and ought to attend class more frequently.
    B) Janie's professor told her that she should find a better place to study, she needed to spend less time visiting with her friends, and she ought to attend class more frequently.
    C) Janie's professor told her that she should find a better place to study, less time visiting with her friends, and ought to attend class more frequently.
    D) Janie's professor told her that she should find a better place to study, spend less time visiting with her friends, and she ought to attend class more frequently.
    E) Janie's professor told her that she should find a better place to study, spend less time visiting with her friends, and she might try to attend class more frequently.

66. I have not forgot the work that I promised to do.

    A) I have not forgot
    B) I will not forgot
    C) I have not forget
    D) I will not forgetten
    E) I have not forgotten

67. Cindy claimed that she was unaware of the affect she had on people.

    A) of the affect she had
    B) of the effect she had
    C) of the affects she was having
    D) of the affect she had had
    E) of the effect she have

68. After running for three miles, Gabby decided that she needed to lie down and rest.

    A) that she needed to lie down
    B) that she needed to lay down
    C) that she would need to lay down
    D) that she had need to lie down
    E) to laid down

69. Kaitlin asked her teacher to raise her grade timidly.

    A) Kaitlin asked her teacher to raise her grade timidly.
    B) Timidly Kaitlin asked her teacher to have raised her grade.
    C) Kaitlin timidly asked her teacher to raise her grade.
    D) Kaitlin was timidly having asked her teacher to raise her grade.
    E) Kaitlin asked her teacher to raise her timid grade.

70. To hike the Appalachian Trail, one needs to be knowledgeable about survival as well as excellent physical condition.

    A) To hike the Appalachian Trail, one needs to be knowledgeable about survival as well as excellent physical condition.
    B) To hike the Appalachian Trail, one needs to be knowledgeable about survival, and should be in excellent physical condition.
    C) To hike the Appalachian Trail, one needs to be knowledgeable about survival and should be in excellent physical condition.
    D) To hike the Appalachian Trail, one needs to be knowledgeable about survival, be in excellent physical condition.
    E) To hike the Appalachian Trial, one needs to be knowledgeable about survival, and excellent physical condition.

71. Jonathan told her mother that he was going to do his <u>homework, then he went to</u> his room to do it.

    A) homework, then he went to
    B) homework; then he went to
    C) homework, and then he went to
    D) homework, however then he went to
    E) homework afterwards he went to

72. <u>John swim in the pool</u> with his friends after school on Thursdays.

    A) John swim in the pool
    B) John swum in the pool
    C) John will have swum in the pool
    D) John swims in the pool
    E) John had swimmed in the pool

73. The car already <u>will have been taken</u> to the mechanic.

    A) will have been taken
    B) has been taken
    C) had been took
    D) was took
    E) is taken

74. The <u>Statue of Liberty was a symbol</u> of freedom and hope.

    A) Statue of Liberty was a symbol
    B) Statue of Liberty had been a symbol
    C) Statue of Liberty is a symbol
    D) Statue of Liberty will be a symbol
    E) Statue of Liberty were a symbol

75. Jennika <u>would have preferred to have spoken</u> to her counselor in person.

    A) would have preferred to have spoken
    B) would have preferred to have speaked
    C) would have preferred if she would have spoken
    D) would have preferred to speak
    E) would prefer to have speaken

76. The stage manager <u>asked to who she should complain</u> about the faulty computer system.

    A) asked to who she should complain
    B) asked to that she should complain
    C) asked that she should complain
    D) asked to whom she had complaining
    E) asked to whom she should complain

77. Jennifer admitted to the detective <u>that it was her that had</u> destroyed the crucial evidence.

    A) that it was her that had
    B) that it was she that had
    C) that it was her who had
    D) that it was she who had
    E) that it was she which had

78. The notice posted on the door informed Bethany <u>that it was her responsibility</u> to pay rent within the next two days.

    A) that it was her responsibility
    B) that it was herself responsibility
    C) that it was she responsibility
    D) that it was hers responsibility
    E) that it was she's responsibility

79. The entire committee agreed that <u>Samantha and me</u> should receive a raise this quarter.

    A) Samantha and me
    B) me and Samantha
    C) I and Samantha
    D) Samantha and myself
    E) Samantha and I

80. Everything that the students learn <u>are essential to their</u> future careers.

    A) are essential to their
    B) is essential to their
    C) was essential to they
    D) is essential to they
    E) was essential to their

81. <u>Sam and Jordan's bikes</u> were each bought at the store Bikes 'R' Us.

    A) Sam and Jordan's bikes
    B) Sam and Jordan bike
    C) Sam's and Jordan's bikes
    D) Sam's and Jordan bikes
    E) Sams and Jordans bikes

82. If your teacher tells you that it's <u>acceptable, than you can go</u> to recess early.

    A) acceptable, than you can go
    B) acceptable, then you can go
    C) acceptable then you can go
    D) acceptable than you can go
    E) acceptable, and then you can go

83. <u>Years after their marriage Joan and Jim</u> were still deeply in love.

    A) Years after their marriage Joan and Jim
    B) Years' after their marriage; Joan and Jim
    C) Year's after their marriage, Joan and Jim
    D) Years after their marriage, Joan and Jim
    E) Years' after their marriage. Joan and Jim

84. Many Puerto Rican natives <u>will have emigrated</u> to New York City in the last 50 years.

    A) will have emigrated
    B) will emigrate
    C) would have emigrated
    D) would emigrate
    E) have emigrated

85. Judge Jones must maintain objectivity in this case <u>if he is to make an</u> unbiased decision.

    A) if he is to make an
    B) if he was to make an
    C) if he were to have made an
    D) if he is to made an
    E) if he's making an

86. There were many <u>french emigrations to America</u> following the German invasion.

    A) french emigrations to America
    B) French emigrants to America
    C) french emigrants to america
    D) French emigrations to america
    E) French emigrations to America

87. The downturn in Tonio's career <u>was the affect</u> of his marriage to Consuelo.

    A) was the effect
    B) were the affect
    C) was the effect
    D) had been the affect
    E) was affected

88. <u>GM recalled 48,000 cars in 1998 that recall did not solve the problem</u>.

    A) GM recalled 48,000 cars in 1998 that recall did not solve the problem
    B) GM recalled 48,000 cars in 1998 however that recall did not solve the problem
    C) GM recalled 48,000 cars in 1998, that recall did not solve the problem
    D) GM recalled 48,000 cars in 1998, although that recall did not solve the problem
    E) GM recalled 48,000 cars in 1998, but that recall did not solve the problem

89. Although she knew that the car <u>was to expensive, Kendra</u> decided to buy it.

    A) was to expensive, Kendra
    B) is to expensive; Kendra
    C) was too expensive, Kendra
    D) is too expensive: Kendra
    E) was too expensive Kendra

90. Helen took pain killers to ease her joint pain. During her afternoon <u>walk; however, the</u> pain returned.

    A) walk; however, the
    B) walk, however, the
    C) walk; however; the
    D) walk however the
    E) walk however, the

91. Wolves, originally found all over Europe, are <u>the ancestor's of dogs</u>.

    A) the ancestor's of dogs
    B) the ancestors of dog's
    C) the ancestors' of dogs
    D) the ancestors of dogs
    E) the ancestors of dogs'

92. The Alps have always been European <u>climbers' favorite area</u>.

    A) climbers' favorite area
    B) climbers favorite areas
    C) climber's favorite areas
    D) climbers favorite area
    E) climber's favorite area

93. The three boys insisted that the money, which had been found by <u>the police, be-longs to them</u>.

    A) the police, belongs to them
    B) the police, belongs to him
    C) the police, belonged to them
    D) the police belonging to them
    E) the police belonged to them

94. The attorney told his client to go to the office and give the paperwork <u>to whoever he saw first</u>.

    A) to whoever he saw first
    B) to whomever he saw first
    C) to who he saw first
    D) to whoever his saw first
    E) to whomever he sawed first

95. <u>I can't make it to the bank today, I will cash the check tomorrow</u>.

    A) I can't make it to the bank today, I will cash the check tomorrow
    B) I can't make it to the bank today however I will cash the check tomorrow
    C) I can't make it to the bank today I will cash the check tomorrow
    D) I can't make it to the bank today, although I will cash the check tomorrow
    E) I can't make it to the bank today, so I will cash the check tomorrow

96. The supervisor requested that <u>myself and Derik ensure</u> that the necessary paper-work gets filed.

    A) myself and Derik ensure
    B) Derik and myself ensure
    C) Derik and me insure
    D) Derik and I ensure
    E) me and Derik ensure

97. <u>Danielle went both to</u> the store and the bank after work last Thursday.

    A) Danielle went both to
    B) Danielle went to both
    C) Danielle had gone both to
    D) Danielle will go both to
    E) Danielle with both go to

98. <u>Not only is the family going</u> to Canada, but also to Mexico this summer.

    A) Not only is the family going
    B) Not is the family is going
    C) The not only family is going
    D) Only not the family is going
    E) The family is going not only

99. <u>The girl watching her television</u> when she heard the news about the fire.

    A) The girl watching her television
    B) The girl will have been watching her television
    C) The girl was watching her television
    D) The girl were watching her television
    E) The girl would watch her television

100. Before one goes to the store one should be sure <u>that your car is working properly</u>.

    A) that your car is working properly
    B) that you're car is working properly
    C) that one's car is working properly
    D) that one's cars are working properly
    E) that ones car is working properly

101. The manager <u>required she to fill</u> out a lot of paperwork before checking out for the day.

    A) required she to fill
    B) requires she to fill
    C) required to her fill
    D) required her to fill
    E) her required to fill

102. The first line of the preamble to the Constitution <u>is "We the people".</u>

    A) is "We the people".
    B) was we the people.
    C) is; "We the people".
    D) was, "We the people".
    E) is "We the people."

103. The band had <u>four tubas, nine trumpets, and 23 trombones</u>.

    A) four tubas, nine trumpets, and 23 trombones
    B) 4 tubas, 9 trumpets, and 23 trombones
    C) 4 tubas, nine trumpets, and 23 trombones
    D) four tubas, nine trumpets and twenty-three trombones
    E) four tubas, 9 trumpets, and 23 trombones

104. He asked me <u>whether or not I wanted to go to dinner?</u>

    A) whether or not I wanted to go to dinner?
    B) whether or not I wanted to have gone to dinner?
    C) whether or not I would've wished to go to dinner?
    D) whether or not I wanted to go to dinner.
    E) whether I wished to have gone to dinner or not.

105. <u>Everyone at Janie's party were going</u> to eat pizza for dinner.

    A) Everyone at Janie's party were going
    B) Everyone at Janies party were to go
    C) Everyone at Janie's party was going
    D) Everyone at Janies' party was going
    E) Everyone at Janie's party had been going

106. Something that the suspect said kept echoing in the detective's mind, and he was sure that <u>it's an important detail</u>.

   A) it's an important detail
   B) its an important detail
   C) its' an important detail
   D) it had been an important detail
   E) it was an important detail

107. Although it was frigid, the ocean <u>was blue and inviting, and members</u> of the Polar Bear club jumped in with enthusiasm.

   A) was blue and inviting, and members
   B) is blue and inviting, and members
   C) was blue and inviting, and member's
   D) is blue and inviting, and member's
   E) was blue, and inviting, and members

108. <u>The evening had made me light-headed and happy, I think I walked into a deep sleep as I entered my front door.</u>

   A) The evening had made me light-headed and happy, I think I walked in a deep sleep as I entered my front door.
   B) The evening had made me light-headed and happy I think I walked in a deep sleep as I entered my front door.
   C) The evening had made me light-headed and happy; I think I walked in a deep sleep as I entered my front door.
   D) The evening had made me light-headed, and happy, I think I walked in a deep sleep, as I entered my front door.
   E) The evening had made me light-headed, happy; I think I walked in a deep sleep as I entered my front door.

109. <u>As a young girl, Bobby walked me to school.</u>

   A) As a young girl, Bobby walked me to school
   B) As a young girl, then Bobby walked me to school
   C) As a young girl, Bobby was walking me to school
   D) As a young girl I was often walked to school by Bobby
   E) Bobby, as a young girl, walked me to school

110. The man was a masterful <u>painter, sculptor, and was good at art</u>.

    A) painter, sculptor, and was good at art
    B) painter, sculptor, and artist
    C) painter, sculptor, and was a wonderful drawer
    D) painter, sculptor, and could draw well
    E) painter and sculptor and artist

111. Jamison <u>would have liked to have continued eating</u> the pie, but it was all gone.

    A) would have liked to have continued eating
    B) would have liked to continue having eaten
    C) would have liked to eat
    D) would have liked to have continue eating
    E) would have liked to continue eating

112. Joan <u>was sure happy that</u> he had passed the test.

    A) was sure happy that
    B) is sure happy when
    C) was surely happy that
    D) is certainly happy when
    E) was surely happy because that

113. After making popcorn, <u>John preceded to watch</u> the movie.

    A) John preceded to watch
    B) John precedes to watch
    C) John is preceding to watch
    D) John proceeded to watch
    E) John proceeding to watch

114. While she was doing the dishes, <u>Jessica layed her folder on</u> the counter.

    A) Jessica layed her folder on
    B) Jessica lain her folder on
    C) Jessica lays her folder on
    D) Jessica will lay her folder on
    E) Jessica laid her folder on

115. The girls argued that the money <u>was really theirs</u>, not their mother's.

    A) was really theirs
    B) was really they'res
    C) was really theres
    D) was really theres
    E) was really there's

116. <u>Daisy and Tom were sitting opposite each other at the kitchen table; with a plate of cold fried chicken between them and two bottles of ale.</u>

    A) Daisy and Tom were sitting opposite each other at the kitchen table; with a plate of cold fried chicken between them and two bottles of ale.
    B) Daisy and Tom were sitting opposite each other at the kitchen table with a plate of cold fried chicken between them and two bottles of ale.
    C) Daisy and Tom were sitting opposite each other at the kitchen table with a plate of cold fried chicken between them; and two bottles of ale.
    D) Daisy and Tom were sitting opposite each other, at the kitchen table with a plate of cold fried chicken between them, and two bottles of ale.
    E) Daisy and Tom were sitting, opposite of each other, at the kitchen tables with a plate of cold, fried, chicken between them, and two bottles of ale.

117. The mothers were all pleased <u>because their child's school was immaculate</u> after the cleaning crew finished.

    A) because their child's school was immaculate
    B) because there child's school was immaculate
    C) because their children's school was immaculate
    D) because they're children's school was immaculate
    E) because their children's school is immaculate

118. The mayor went to the meeting <u>and tells the board that they needed</u> to increase funding for the school system in the next year.

    A) and tells the board that they needed
    B) and told the board that they need
    C) and told the board that they had needed
    D) and told the board that they needed
    E) and tells the board that they need

119. <u>Neither the teacher or the principal</u> was aware that the student had a peanut allergy.

   A) Neither the teacher or the principal
   B) Neither the teacher and the principal
   C) Neither the teacher but the principal
   D) Neither the teacher, the principal
   E) Neither the teacher nor the principal

120. The students were all elated when Mrs.Janis <u>decided to by a animal for</u> a class pet.

   A) decided to by a animal for
   B) decided to buy a animal for
   C) decided to buy an animal for
   D) decided to by an animal for
   E) decides to buy an animal for

121. The three girls got in an argument over the slices of pie because <u>there were only to left in the pan</u>.

   A) there were only to left in the pan
   B) there were only two left in the pan
   C) there were only too left in the pan
   D) their were only two left in the pan
   E) there only were two left in the pan

122. The hospital <u>spent 25,000,000 dollars</u> on a new piece of equipment.

   A) spent 25,000,000 dollars
   B) spended 25,000,000 dollars
   C) spented 25 million dollars
   D) spent 25 million dollars
   E) spent twenty-five million dollars

123. The company assured the clients that <u>your personal information would not be disclosed</u>.

   A) your personal information would not be disclosed
   B) our personal information would not be disclosed
   C) their personal information would not be closed
   D) your personal information would not have been disclosed
   E) their personal information would not have been disclosed

124. Everyone was aghast <u>when they learned that Mr. Jones was the killer</u>.

     A) when they learned that Mr. Jones was the killer
     B) before they had learned that Mr. Jones was the killer
     C) when they had learned that Mr. Jones were the killer
     D) after they learn that Mr. Jones was the killer
     E) if they learned that Mr. Jones was the killer

125. <u>Every student in the room ran to pick up their backpack</u>.

     A) Every student in the room ran to pick up their backpack
     B) Everyone student in the room ran to pick up their backpack
     C) All students on the room ran to pick up their backpack
     D) Everyone student in the room ran to pick up his/her backpack
     E) Every student in the room ran to pick up his/her backpack

126. Shortly after the doctor <u>saw the patient, they determined</u> a suitable diagnosis.

     A) saw the patient, they determined
     B) saw the patient they determined
     C) saw the patient, he determined
     D) saw the patient; he determined
     E) saw the patient he determined

127. After going to <u>the store with her mother, Jen asked</u> her to drop her off at her apartment.

     A) the store with her mother, Jen asked
     B) the store with her mother. Jen asked
     C) the store with her mother: Jen will have asked
     D) the store from her mother, Jen asked
     E) the store with her mother Jen asked

128. Martha asked her doctor whether or not he <u>was sure that she had cancer?</u>

     A) was sure that she had cancer?
     B) was surely that she had cancer?
     C) was sure about that she had cancer.
     D) was sure that she had cancer.
     E) was sure which she had cancer.

129. My professor <u>asked me and Amber</u> to help him with his research next semester.

    A) asked me and Amber
    B) asked I and Amber
    C) asked Amber and myself
    D) asked Amber and I
    E) asked Amber and me

130. I decided to <u>clean my room myself because</u> my roommate did not want to help me.

    A) clean my room myself because
    B) clean my room myself, because
    C) clean my room herself, because
    D) clean my room herself because
    E) clean my room mineself because

131. <u>Samantha was real glad that</u> her mother was there when she got her high school diploma.

    A) Samantha was real glad that
    B) Samantha was really glad that
    C) Samantha was real gladly that
    D) Samantha was really gladly that
    E) Samantha was real sure glad that

132. The ski resort <u>had less customers during the summer</u> months than in the winter months.

    A) had less customers during the summer
    B) had less customer's during the summer
    C) had less customers during the Summer
    D) had fewer customer's during the summer
    E) had fewer customers during the summer

133. She is going not only to the <u>conference in the morning, but to the lunch</u> in the afternoon.

    A) conference in the morning, but to the lunch
    B) conference in the morning, and also to the lunch
    C) conference in the morning, but also to the lunch
    D) conference in the morning, but also the lunch
    E) conference in the morning, and also the lunch

134. <u>Sean and myself went</u> to the retreat at the specific request of our manager.

    A) Sean and myself went
    B) Sean and me went
    C) Me and Sean went
    D) Sean and I went
    E) Myself and Sean went

135. I do not want to go <u>to the store, I want</u> to go to the park.

    A) to the store, I want
    B) to the store, but I want
    C) to the store I want
    D) to the store – I wanted
    E) to the stores, I wanted

136. Despite his many <u>years of training; however, Dr. Jonathan</u> did not know how to treat the patient.

    A) years of training; however, Dr. Jonathan
    B) year's of training; however, Dr. Jonathan
    C) years of training, however, Dr. Jonathan
    D) year's of training, however, Dr. Jonathan
    E) years of training however Dr. Jonathan

137. It's important to find a job that you enjoy doing <u>so that one will have a happy life</u>.

    A) so that one will have a happy life
    B) so that one's will have a happy lifes
    C) so which you will have a happy life
    D) so that you will have had a happy life
    E) so that you will have a happy life

138. <u>Christopher going to the</u> store to buy some candy after school.

    A) Christopher going to the
    B) Christopher is going to the
    C) Christopher will going to the
    D) Christopher can going to the
    E) Christopher has going to the

139. Mandi wants to go to the management conference <u>because it has looked good on her application</u> to business school.

    A) because it has looked good on her application
    B) because it has looked well on her application
    C) because it will look good on her application
    D) because it will looked well on her application
    E) because it will have looked good on her application

140. The airline <u>ticket is purchased</u> after the family arrived at the airport.

    A) ticket is purchased
    B) ticket will be purchased
    C) ticket has been purchased
    D) ticket will have been purchased
    E) ticket was purchased

141. It was gratifying for the athlete to know that after her many years of training, <u>she would finally be competing</u> in the next Olympics.

    A) she would finally be competing
    B) she would finally be compete
    C) she was finally being competing
    D) she had finally been competing
    E) she would finally have competed

142. <u>The dog's collar was a fancy one, and it</u> shocked him whenever he got too far from the house.

    A) The dog's collar was a fancy one, and it
    B) The dogs collar was a fancy one, and it
    C) The dogs collar was a fancy one and it
    D) The dog's collar was a fancy one and it
    E) The dog's dollar was a fancy one; and it

143. <u>Sobbing uncontrollably, the doctor told the patient that he had cancer.</u>

    A) Sobbing uncontrollably, the doctor told the patient that he had cancer.
    B) The doctor, sobbing uncontrollably, told the patient that he had cancer.
    C) The doctor told the patient that he was sobbing uncontrollably and had cancer.
    D) The doctor told the patient, who was sobbing uncontrollably, that he had cancer.
    E) Sobbing uncontrollably, the patient told the doctor that he had cancer.

144. <u>The team who won</u> the conference would be going to the international competition next spring.

    A) The team who won
    B) The team who had won
    C) The team that won
    D) The team that which had won
    E) The team that winning

145. <u>The teacher's held</u> a meeting that morning to discuss the upcoming school assembly.

    A) The teacher's held
    B) The teacher held
    C) The teachers will held
    D) The teacher's would have hold
    E) The teachers held

146. Everything that the supervisor taught <u>the trainees were important</u> to their daily work.

    A) the trainees were important
    B) the trainees was important
    C) the trainee's were important
    D) the trainee's was important
    E) the trainees will have been important

147. <u>There are 26 letters in the alphabet</u>, and they form the words which we speak each day.

    A) There are 26 letters in the alphabet
    B) There are twenty-six letters in the alphabet
    C) There are 26-letters in the alphabet
    D) There are twenty 6 letters in the alphabet
    E) There are 20 six letters in the alphabet

148. Jordan had hoped that failing his first-year writing <u>class would not effect his chances</u> at getting into law school.

    A) class would not effect his chances
    B) class will not effect his chances
    C) class would not affect his chances
    D) class will not affect his chances
    E) class would not have affected his chances

149. My mother asked me to make sure that the <u>decision to attend college was mine own</u>.

    A) decision to attend college was mine own
    B) decision to attend college was my own
    C) decision to attend college was myselfs
    D) decision to attending college were mine own
    E) decision to attend college were my own

150. The detective felt that it was his personal responsibility to discover <u>whom's</u> fault the murder was.

    A) whom's
    B) whom
    C) who's
    D) whose
    E) whomevers

SECTION 2 ANSWER KEY

1. B	42. B	83. D	124. A
2. E	43. A	84. E	125. E
3. A	44. D	85. A	126. C
4. B	45. E	86. B	127. A
5. D	46. A	87. C	128. D
6. E	47. C	88. E	129. E
7. B	48. E	89. C	130. A
8. C	49. B	90. B	131. B
9. A	50. D	91. D	132. E
10. D	51. B	92. A	133. C
11. E	52. B	93. C	134. D
12. A	53. E	94. B	135. B
13. A	54. A	95. E	136. C
14. B	55. D	96. D	137. E
15. C	56. C	97. B	138. B
16. C	57. B	98. E	139. C
17. E	58. D	99. C	140. E
18. B	59. D	100. C	141. A
19. A	60. A	101. D	142. A
20. C	61. B	102. E	143. D
21. D	62. C	103. B	144. C
22. D	63. E	104. D	145. E
23. B	64. A	105. C	146. B
24. E	65. B	106. E	147. A
25. C	66. E	107. A	148. C
26. E	67. B	108. C	149. B
27. B	68. A	109. D	150. D
28. C	69. C	110. B	
29. D	70. C	111. E	
30. E	71. C	112. C	
31. A	72. D	113. D	
32. B	73. B	114. E	
33. C	74. C	115. A	
34. E	75. D	116. B	
35. C	76. E	117. C	
36. D	77. D	118. D	
37. B	78. A	119. E	
38. E	79. E	120. C	
39. C	80. B	121. B	
40. E	81. C	122. D	
41. A	82. C	123. D	

Section 3: Improving Paragraphs

SENTENCE VARIETY

When you were young and just learning to talk, you often said things in the simplest way possible. You might have a conversation at night with your parents that went something like this: "Today I went to school, and I had recess, and I played with my friends. Then I came home, and I had a snack. And I played kickball with Sandy. Then I took a bath and went to bed."

Can you imagine reading a novel that sounded like a first-grade conversation? That's how writing would sound if all your sentences were the same, or if they were all simple or compound sentences. Learning how to incorporate different styles and different lengths of sentences vastly improves the quality of writing.

Incorporate various simple, compound, complex, and compound-complex sentences in writing to give variety and make the writing more interesting. It is also helpful to incorporate different writing strategies such as comparisons, parallel syntax, and others to improve writing quality.

Remember that word and sentence length had nothing to do with the correctness of a sentence. Good writers vary the length of their sentences, intermingling short, emphatic sentences with longer, more complex ones. You may want to count the number of words in each sentence on a page. If they are all approximately the same, you'll need to work on combining some sentences, shortening some, experimenting with different punctuation, and making sure that you raise the level of writing to a college-level sophistication by creating variety.

COMPARISONS

One of the most effective ways to describe or explain something is by using comparisons. When writing it is important that all comparisons are clear, logical, easy to understand, and parallel in structure. Some of the most basic types of comparisons are similes, metaphors, and analogies.

Analogy: A comparison between two things on a basis of their similarity.

Simile: A comparison using *like* or *as*.

Metaphor: A direct comparison, often using *is* to describe something.

That comparisons must be parallel in structure refers to the construction of the description. In order to clarify analogies, the same phrases should be used with each element.

> UNPARALLEL: She had always expressed more interest in writing than dancing.
> CORRECT: She had always expressed more interesting in writing than she had in dancing.

> UNCLEAR: The engine on the Ford truck was better than the Chevy.
> CORRECT: The engine on the Ford truck was better than the engine on the Chevy.

> UNCLEAR and UNPARALLEL: His parents were wealthier than smart.
> CORRECT: His parents had more money than they had intelligence.

There are a couple of phrases that you need to specifically look out for when making comparisons that are referred to as connectives. These are pairs of phrases that always go together:

- Not only / but also
- Both / and
- Either / or
- Neither / nor

If a comparison is long or contains more than one element continue repeating the phrase to ensure that it is parallel throughout the comparison.

> WRONG: **Not only** is she going to California this summer, **but** to New York.
> CORRECT: **Not only** is she going to California this summer, **but also** to New York.

> WRONG: I prefer this grocery store because it is **both** near my house **or** well stocked.
> CORRECT: I prefer this grocery store because it is **both** near my house **and** well stocked.

> WRONG: **Either** she should get a job, she should get an internship, she should do a study abroad.
> CORRECT: **Either** <u>she should</u> get a job **or** <u>she should</u> get an internship or she should do a study abroad.

> WRONG: **Neither** the cat **or** the dog is allowed to eat at the table.
> CORRECT: **Neither** the cat **nor** the dog is allowed to eat at the table.

COHERENCE

Coherency and logic within each paragraph is just as important as coherency within sentences and within the paper as a whole. This means that the relationship between each individual sentence should be clear. Furthermore, each sentence in any particular paragraph should be connected to the main idea or "topic sentence" of that paragraph. If there is extra information in a paragraph, it should either be moved to a different paragraph or a new paragraph should be started to ensure that all of the information is organized logically.

One of the best ways to create coherence within paragraphs is to use transition to show your train of thought from one sentence to the next. For example, some common transitions include

- Again
- Also
- Anyway
- As a result
- As soon as
- Besides
- Certainly
- Even though
- Finally
- For example
- Furthermore
- Granted that
- However
- In addition
- In conclusion
- In the meantime
- Indeed
- Instead
- Likewise
- Etc.

Another method of creating coherence within a paragraph is to repeat or reiterate key words throughout the paragraph. Concentrate on varying the words so that you don't repeat the same exact word over and over, but rather that you reiterate the "meaning" of the idea through different words.

Consider the following paragraph taken from an essay entitled "Computers Inspire Fear, Fascination." The author uses the key themes of "Native Americans" and "computers" in several ways throughout the paragraph, giving it coherence.

"Like the <u>Native Americans</u> watching <u>invaders</u> with fear and fascination, I observe the influx of computers into our society. Little did the <u>Native Americans</u> know that their world would be irrevocably changed and their very being would be endangered. Little do we know yet about how humanity will be affected by the mighty <u>computer</u>, and we're left to wonder if the cost of <u>technology</u> is the price of genuine communication."

Notice how the paragraph also gains coherence for the proper use of the analogy between Native Americans and the European infiltration of land with the infusion of computers into modern society. Continued analogy, such as this, is another way to hold ideas together.

LANGUAGE

Words! Words! Words! Your paper (and your grade) is built on the power of the written word. In a College Composition class you can't, after all, "talk" your papers out loud. To improve your writing, follow the listed strategies:

1. Your paper should always sound like you, not a textbook. In the world of writing, sounding like yourself, a real person, is called "voice." Utilizing your "voice" doesn't mean that you can't be the best you can be and use powerful prose. It simply means that you don't need to use a thesaurus on every other word.

2. Use descriptive words.
    Thoroughly consider the alternate word choices. For instance, consider the number of words that would more accurately portray the meaning of "said:" *Declared, demanded, uttered, muttered, whispered, shouted, retorted, replied, answered, croaked, theorized, responded, debated, pleaded, begged, laughed –* to name just a few.

3. In general, it's better to use one strong word than two weak ones:
    "The baby wailed" instead of "The baby cried loudly."
    "The man whooped" instead of "The man laughed suddenly."

4. Avoid clichés, the worn-out old sayings.
    Make new comparisons that are fresh and unique:
    Not "white as snow," but "white as an albino cotton ball."

5. Don't utilize "sexist" language. Many people object to the traditional male pronoun to indicate everyone. Words like "mailman," and "fireman" should be changed to "mail carrier" and "firefighter." In order to avoid sentences where you have to use a male pronoun, use the plural form:
    NOT: "A doctor must find an office before he can set up a practice."
    BUT: "Doctors must find office space before they can set up practice."

EVALUATION OF REASONING

Two main types of reasoning exist and are used to convince or persuade:

1. Inductive reasoning occurs when a generalization is made based on a number of specific instances.
    "I have ridden a roller coaster a dozen times in the last year, and every single time, I've gotten sick after the ride stopped."
    Inductive reasoning would say that based on a specific number of instances, the general statement could be made:
    "Riding roller coasters makes me sick."

2. Deductive reasoning occurs when a general principle is applied to a specific case.
    "Because riding roller coasters makes me sick, trips on 'the Teacup' will also make me sick." Deductive reasoning is much trickier than inductive because there are often no definitive answers. The reader must agree with the major statement in the first part of the deduction.

When evaluating the reasoning of an argument, make sure that each part of a statement is true, and that all claims are backed up by some kind of evidence.

POINT OF VIEW

When you write, you may opt to use the *first person point-of-view,* I or we.

The *second person point-of-view* is using "you." (Before you utilize the word "you," addressing the reader on an informal basis, clarify with your instructor whether or not he/she allows that kind of informality.)

The *third person point-of-view* means using the pronouns, "he, she, it, or they."

Whatever point-of-view you choose, be consistent.

"The entire continuum of care exists under one roof. A leader in cancer education, the Cancer Center has served the area for more than a decade. The Center has a full staff of registered doctors and nurses to aid our patients. We have a special treatment room where you can watch television as your chemotherapy is being delivered. The staff is caring and compassionate, and they are all Board Certified. "

Notice the inconsistencies between the use of the point of view from "the Cancer Center" (it) to "we," and "they," as well as the switch from the word "patients" to "you." Pick a point-of-view and stick with it!

WRITING PARAGRAPHS

TRIAC: Paragraph and Paper Organization
TRIAC is a writing strategy you can use for each paragraph to create a solid organization and an effective argument. TRIAC stands for:

T	Topic Sentence - The first sentence introduces the subject of a paragraph, and serves as a "minor" thesis statement.
R	Restatement or Restriction - The second sentence can restate or restrict what was written in the first sentence, making the subject more specific.
I	Illustration - This section of the paragraph consists of the illustrations (evidence, data, facts, quotes, etc.) that support your topic sentence. This section can contain several sentences.
A	Analysis - Explain, interpret, and contextualize the illustrations that have been made. Illustrations are not effective without the writer analyzing them.
C	Conclusion - The final sentence (or two) might review what the paragraph has discussed, and/or reemphasize what the illustration and analysis suggest. This closing section may also evaluate the connections you've made in your paragraph. You are setting yourself up to move smoothly and logically into the next paragraph.

Sample Questions – Test Yourself

Use the following passage to answer the sample test questions:

(1) Prom time and hero worship are inevitably linked in my mind. (2) Being five years younger than my sister, Melanie, I was always in awe of her friends. (3) I know now that the magic of youth and the love of my sister colored her friends with the glow of heroism. (4) But to this day, one of these people still withstands the test of time. (5) Every spring, I think of Tommy Nolan, a hero whose image will never tarnish.

(6) I don't remember much of the courtship between Melanie and Tommy except his first impromptu visit to the Johnson household. (7) On a warm spring when he first dropped by after baseball practice, my sister was cooking dinner and waiting for my parents to return from work. (8) Never a very attentive cook and flustered by his visit, Melanie burnt the potatoes and steak. (9) Of course, my father picked that day to ask Tommy to stay for dinner. (10) He almost made my sister die of embarrassment.

(11) That afternoon, my parents, who were militarily strict when it came to dating and boys, developed an early affection for Tommy. (12) Who, after all, couldn't love a guy who munched black steak and said that his steak was "crunchy"?

1. Which of the following is the best way to combine line 3 and 4?

   A) I know now that the magic of youth and the love of my sister colored her friends with the glow of heroism. And to this day, one of those people still withstands the test of time.
   B) I know now that the magic of youth and the love of my sister colored her friends with the glow of heroism, but to this day, one of those people still withstands the test of time.
   C) I know now that the magic of youth and the love of my sister colored her friends with the glow of heroism; in addition, to this day, one of those people still withstands the test of time.
   D) I know now that the magic of youth and the love of my sister colored her friends with the glow of heroism; therefore, one of those people still withstands the test of time.
   E) I know now that the magic of youth and the love of my sister colored her friends with the glow of heroism, so to this day, one of those people still withstands the test of time.

2. Which of the following possibilities best adds descriptive language to line 8?

   A) Never a very attentive cook and flustered by his visit, Melanie burnt the potatoes and steak black.
   B) Never a very attentive cook and flustered by his visit, Melanie burnt the potatoes to a blackened film on the pan and the steak.
   C) Never a very attentive cook and flustered by his visit, Melanie burnt the potatoes to a blackened film on the pan and the steak was crunchy.
   D) Never a very attentive cook and flustered by his visit, Melanie burnt the potatoes to a smelly blank and burned steak.
   E) Never a very attentive cook and flustered by his visit, Melanie burnt the potatoes to a blackened film on the pan and broiled the steak to a charcoal.

3. Which of the following possibilities best combines lines 9 and 10?

   A) Of course, my father picked that day to ask Tommy to stay for dinner almost causing death-by-embarrassment for my sister.
   B) Of course, my father picked that day to ask Tommy to stay for dinner, he almost made my sister die of embarrassment.
   C) Of course, my father picked that day to ask Tommy to stay of dinner, and my sister had embarrassment.
   D) Of course, my father picked that day to ask Tommy to stay for dinner, since he almost made my sister die of embarrassment.
   E) Of course, my father picked that day to ask Tommy to stay for dinner ; although my sister was dying from embarrassment.

4. Which of the following possibilities for line 12 most effectively depicts the incident?

   A) Who, after all, couldn't love a guy who munched black steak and said that he liked it crunchy.
   B) Who, after all, couldn't love a guy who munched black steak and said that he liked it this way.
   C) Who, after all, couldn't love a guy who munched black steak and said, "I like my meat a little crunchy?"
   D) Who, after all, couldn't love a guy who munched black and said that he ate it crunchy.
   E) Who, after all, couldn't love a guy who munched black steak and says that he likes it crunchy.

5. The passage is written in which point of view?

    A) Third person plural
    B) Second person plural
    C) Third person singular
    D) Second person singular
    E) First person singular

6. Which of the following writing strategies does NOT appear in the passage?

    A) Point of view
    B) Compare/contrast
    C) Descriptive language
    D) Parallel structure
    E) Chronological order

7. Which line should be omitted from the passage?

    A) Line 1
    B) Line 4
    C) Line 7
    D) Line 9
    E) Line 12

8. Line 12 is written in which tense?

    A) Present tense
    B) Present-perfect tense
    C) Past tense
    D) Future tense
    E) Past-perfect tense

9. The following line would most logically be inserted where into the passage?

    Years later, when Melanie saw Tommy again, she said if you looked into his eyes they were still the kind, gentle, green eyes of the teenager who had captured her heart.

    A) After line 3
    B) After line 6
    C) After line 8
    D) After line 10
    E) After line 12

10. In context, the word "colored" in line 3 can best be interpreted to mean

    A) An art project
    B) Hid
    C) Upset
    D) To make appear in a certain way
    E) A reference to skin tone

SAMPLE QUESTION KEY – TEST YOURSELF

    1. B
    2. E
    3. A
    4. C
    5. D
    6. B
    7. A
    8. C
    9. E
    10. D

SECTION 3: PARAGRAPH IMPROVEMENT QUESTIONS

Questions 1-7 are based on the following passage:

(1) By 1806 Napoleon had managed to conquer most of mainland Europe, he moved his attention to Britain. (2) The recent destruction of his navy meant that was not feasible for him to launch an actual attack, and instead he turned to an economic solution termed the Continental System.

(3) The purpose of the Continental System was to cut off Britain from foreign trade and aid. (4) As a mercantile country, Napoleon would then have the upper hand. (5) Another country would therefore be brought under French control without French forces having to fire a shot. (6) French guns were made by German manufacturers.

(7) The system was fairly effective in the sense that it did cause inflation and bankruptcies in Britain. (8) However, it also had negative impacts on French businesses. (9) Within a few years Napoleon was forced to allow trade with Britain to resume in an effort to raise gold which he desperately needed.

1. Where should the following line be inserted into the passage?

   It ordered an embargo of all British goods by France and any countries under its control.

   A) After line 2
   B) Before line 7
   C) After line 3
   D) Before line 1
   E) After line 8

The correct answer is C:) After line 3. Line 3 introduces the purpose of the Continental System, so following line 3 makes it the most logical place to clarify what it does.

2. This passage has which type of organization?

   A) Least important to most important
   B) Chronological
   C) Compare/contrast
   D) Spatial
   E) None of the above

The correct answer is B:) Chronological. The passage describes the effects of the Continental System over time. Therefore, the organization is chronological.

3. What revision must be made to sentence 4?

   A) As a mercantile country, Napoleon would then have the upper hand.
   B) This was ruinous for a mercantile country and Napoleon had the upper hand.
   C) France, a mercantile nation, would be devastated and Napoleon would have the upper hand.
   D) As a mercantile country Napoleon would, then have the upper hand.
   E) This would ruin Britain, a mercantile country, and give Napoleon the upper hand.

The correct answer is E:) This would ruin Britain, a mercantile country, and give Napoleon the upper hand. As written, line 4 contains a dangling modifier. This revision fixes this problem and clarifies the meaning of the line.

4. Which of the following additions to the end paragraph 3 would offer the most improvement?

   A) The Continental System was a low point of Napoleon's long-term war strategy, and in the end was more harmful than it was helpful.
   B) Other countries did not support the embargo, so Napoleon forced them into submission.
   C) Since this time, France and Britain have become strong allies and trading partners in terms of the world market.
   D) France had succeeded in subjugating many of the surrounding nations.
   E) An embargo is an order to cease trade, and in this case was an unsuccessful strategy.

The correct answer is A:) The Continental System was a low point of Napoleon's long-term war strategy, and in the end was more harmful than it was helpful. Paragraph 3 finishes describing the results of the Continental System. Option A is most appropriate because it summarizes the system and makes a nice conclusion to the passage.

5. Which sentence should be omitted?

   A) 1
   B) 3
   C) 5
   D) 6
   E) 8

The correct answer is D:) 6. The focus of the passage is the Continental System. Sentence 6 introduces irrelevant information.

6. Which of the following is the most grammatically correct way to combine lines 7 and 8 (reproduced below)?

(7) The system was fairly effective in the sense that it did cause inflation and bankruptcies in Britain. (8) However, it also had negative impacts on French businesses.

    A) The system was fairly effective in the sense that it did cause inflation and bankruptcies in Britain, however, it also had negative impacts on French businesses.

    B) The system was fairly effective in the sense that it did cause inflation and bankruptcy in Britain, it had negative impacts on French businesses.

    C) The system was fairly effective because it caused inflation and bankruptcies in Britain, and it had negative impacts on French businesses.

    D) The system was fairly effective because it caused inflation and bankruptcy in Britain: on the other hand, it too had negative impacts on French businesses.

    E) The system was fairly effective because it caused inflation and bankruptcies in Britain; however, it also harmed French businesses.

The correct answer is E:) The system was fairly effective because it caused inflation and bankruptcies in Britain; however, it harmed French businesses. Answers A and B are incorrect because a comma cannot join to lines without the additional presence of a conjunction. Answer C is incorrect because it incorrectly indicates that the system was successful because it hurt French businesses. Answer D is incorrect because the colon is used inappropriately.

7. What revision must be made to of sentence 2?

The recent destruction of his navy meant that was not feasible for him to launch an actual attack, and instead he turned to an economic solution termed the Continental System.

    A) It should be moved to the third paragraph

    B) "meant that" should be changed to "meant that it"

    C) "economic" should be changed to "military"

    D) The comma should be replaced with a colon

    E) It should be split into three sentences to ensure that no run-ons occur

The correct answer is B:) "meant that" should be changed to "meant that it." Answer C is incorrect because it is an economic solution. Answer D is incorrect because the comma and coordinating conjunction "and" can be used to join the two independent clauses. Answer E is incorrect because the sentence is not a run-on.

Questions 8-13 are based on the following passage:

(1) All companies must borrow money at some point, and the question that they must answer is whether to seek short-term or long-term financing. (2) Short-term financing is useful for short-term situations. (3) It is often easier to obtain and has a lower total cost than long term financing.

(4) A business could use short term financing if they have cash flow problems, for example. (5) In this case they would just need some extra cash until their money from sales came in, so the need would be immediate and quickly resolved. (6) If a business is incurring temporary or short term costs they may also consider short-term financing like an accounting firm will have a lot of extra work during tax season and may hire temporary employees. (7) They could use short-term financing to pay them.

(8) Long-term financing, on the other hand, is useful for long-term problems. (9) Sources of long-term financing are stocks, bonds, and long-term loans from banks. (10) Long-term financing has lasting impacts on the company, but can be necessary and useful.

(11) For example, long-term financing would be used to fund major projects. (12) For example, if a small family owned hotel wished to expand into a large chain. (13) Long-term financing is also used in funding the procurement of fixed capital, such as new machines, for which the expense is incurred only once. (14) The costs of a keeping a donut shop running may require some sort of financing.

8. This passage has which type of organization?

    A) Chronological
    B) Geographical
    C) Compare/contrast
    D) 5x5
    E) Least important to most important

The correct answer is C:) Compare/contrast. The passage describes the differences between two different types of financing: long-term and short-term.

9. The line below would make the most sense if inserted where into the passage?

Some examples of short-term financing include short-term loans and trade credit (buying inventory on account from suppliers).

A) Before line 1
B) After line 3
C) Before line 5
D) After line 10
E) Before line 13

The correct answer is B:) After line 3. The line belongs in the first part of the passage because this is where short-term financing is described. Therefore, answers D and E can be eliminated. It would be illogical to begin the passage with examples, so option A can be eliminated.

10. Which of the following run-on sentence?

A) 13
B) 11
C) 9
D) 8
E) 6

The correct answer is E:) 6. Line 6 has two different subjects and verbs, and contains a comparison. However, no punctuation or conjunctions are used.

11. Which of the following changes would do the most to clarify line 7?

A) Move it to the end of the third paragraph
B) Add "because it is an immediate need" to the end of the line
C) Change "They" to "The company"
D) Insert "If this were the case" at the beginning of the line
E) Combine it with line 8

The correct answer is C:) Change "They" to "The company." Because two pronouns – they and them – are used, the references become unclear. Changing "They" to "The company" creates specification.

12. Which line should be omitted?

    A) 2
    B) 4
    C) 7
    D) 9
    E) 14

The correct answer is E:) 14. Line 14 is an inappropriate concluding sentence. If it were to be in the passage at all it should be nearer the beginning where the passage is describing the need for financing. Mention of a donut shop is also an inappropriate detail.

13. The purpose of the third paragraph is to

    A) Introduce and describe the second form of financing
    B) Present an argument and its resolution
    C) Discuss a contradictory theory which will later be refuted
    D) Offer the solution to the dilemma presented in paragraph one
    E) Give examples of the subject presented in the second paragraph

The correct answer is A:) Introduce and describe the second form of financing. The third paragraph describes long-term financing. Answer E can be eliminated, therefore, because the paragraph describes a new subject. Options B and D can be eliminated because the passage is informational and does not present a problem.

Questions 14-19 are based on the following passage:

(1) The Kansas City Preventative Patrol Experiment was an experiment carried out in 1970 with the goal of determining the effect that the presence of a marked police car had on crime. (2) The study specifically looked at the rates of crimes and the opinion of the public. (3) The study found that having routine patrols carried out by marked police vehicles did not reduce the amount of crime that was occurring, and it did not have any effects on the public's general feeling of security. (4) It concluded that resources should be allocated away from patrol problems and be placed where they could be more effectively used.
(5) The Kansas City Patrol Experiment was also an important experiment because it demonstrated that there are ethical, effective, and safe ways to carry out experiments relating to police work. (6) The experiment did this because it was carefully designed. (7) Officers to carry out their regular duties while still gaining valuable insights about police work.

14. Which of the following variations of line 1 (reproduced below) is most correct?

The Kansas City Preventative Patrol Experiment was an experiment carried out in 1970 with the goal of determining the effect that the presence of a marked police car had on crime.

A) The Kansas City Preventative Patrol Experiment was an experiment carried out in 1970 with the goal of determining the effect that the presence of a marked police car had on crime.
B) The Kansas City Preventative Patrol Experiment was carried out in 1970 with the goal of determining the effect that the presence of a marked police car has on crime.
C) The Kansas City Preventative Patrol Experiment was an experiment that was carried out in 1970 and did have the goal of determining the effect that the then present marked police cars were having on crime.
D) The effect that the presence of a marked police car had one had on crime has been determine in 1970 and was figured by the Kansas City Preventative Patrol Experiment that has been carried out.
E) The Kansas City Preventative Patrol Experiment determined that marked police cars may or may not effect crime rates.

The correct answer is B:) The Kansas City Preventative Patrol Experiment was carried out in 1970 with the goal of determining the effect that the presence of a marked police car has on crime. Because the effect of police cars on crime is an ongoing fact, it should be referred to in the present tense. Therefore answers A and C can be eliminated. Answer E can be eliminated because "effect" is used incorrectly.

15. Which of the following is a sentence fragment?

    A) 1
    B) 2
    C) 3
    D) 5
    E) 7

The correct answer is E:) 7. Lines 1, 2, 3, and 5 are all complete sentences with both subjects and verbs.

16. "It" in line 4 refers to what?

    A) Marked police cars
    B) The results of the experiment
    C) The general public
    D) Kansas City Preventative Patrol Experiment
    E) A universal truth

The correct answer is D:) Kansas City Preventative Patrol Experiment. Line 3 describes the results of the study, and line 4 continues this.

17. Which of the following BEST summarizes the main idea of the passage?

    A) The Kansas City Preventative Patrol Experiment was important because it both investigated crime and was an effective study.
    B) Marked police cars deter crime.
    C) Police work can be safe.
    D) Studies about crime should not be conducted because they interfere with police work and cannot be definitive.
    E) None of the above

The correct answer is A:) The Kansas City Preventative Patrol Experiment was important because it both investigated crime and was an effective study. Although answers B and C both describe part of the passage, only answer A adequately summarizes the whole passage.

18. The purpose of paragraph 2 is to

A) Reinforce the ideas presented in the first paragraph
B) Offer a second example of the experiment's uses
C) Refute the ideas presented in the first paragraph
D) Present contradictory information
E) Examine the experiment in light of new information

The correct answer is B:) Offer a second example of the experiment's uses. The second paragraph describes that the Kansas City Preventative Patrol Experiment was useful in ways in addition to simply its results. Answer A is therefore incorrect because it introduces new information. Answers C and D are also incorrect because the information does not contradict the initial paragraph, it simply introduces new information.

19. Which of the following revisions must be made?

A) Combine lines 1 and 2 using a semicolon
B) Hyphenate "police work" at the end of line 5
C) Begin line 7 with "It allowed"
D) Change "effect" in line 1 to "affect"
E) No changes should be made

The correct answer is C:) Begin line 7 with "It allowed." As is, line 7 is a sentence fragment. This revision would improve it.

Questions 20-26 are based on the following passage:

(1) The trait-factor theory is a psychological theory that relates to classifying an individual's personality. (2) The basis of the theory is that all individuals can be characterized through a listing of their traits. (3) For example, people understand that a person described as "kind" will be nice and caring and considerate of <u>other's feelings</u>. (4) According to the trait-factor theory, an individual's personality is composed of the compilation of the many traits which describe them.
(5) The trait-factor theory is commonly applied in career counseling. (6) Different types of aptitude tests, or simply general observations of the counselor, are used to determine the traits which the individual best embodies. (7) Alternatively, different career options are also classified by the types of traits which are required to be most successful in that job. (8) The more traits that are common between an individual and a job, the more suited they are to it. (9) Writers should be creative. (10) Therefore, if a person choses a career path which is compatible with their personality traits they will be happier and successful.

20. The following line should be inserted where into the passage?

Traits are relatively stable descriptions of tendencies to act in a certain way.

    A) Before line 1
    B) After line 2
    C) Before line 5
    D) After line 8
    E) Before line 10

The correct answer is B:) After line 2. Line 2 introduces the use of traits in the trait-factor theory. It is therefore logical to define traits at this point.

21. Which of the following changes must be made to line 7?

    A) Insert a comma after "required"
    B) Change "most" to "more"
    C) Change "Alternatively" to "Similarly"
    D) Combine it with line 8
    E) Move it to the end of the first paragraph

The correct answer is C:) Change "Alternatively" to "Similarly." The line describes that both jobs and individuals are described by traits. It is therefore more logical to begin the sentence with "similarly."

22. Which of the following is the best revision of the underlined portion of line 3?

    A) other's feelings
    B) other's feelings'
    C) others feeling's
    D) others feelings
    E) others' feelings

The correct answer is E:) others' feelings. The correct plural form of feeling is feelings with no apostrophe. The word "others'" correctly indicates that there are multiple people, with multiple feelings.

23. Which line should be omitted from the second paragraph?

    A) 6
    B) 7
    C) 8
    D) 9
    E) 10

The correct answer is D:) 9. It is illogical to include line 9 when no other examples of pairing traits and jobs are given, and the paragraph does not refer to writers at any other point either.

24. Which of the following would be the best addition to the passage as a third paragraph?

    A) A paragraph about the factor-trait theory
    B) A paragraph offering examples of traits that match with certain professions
    C) A paragraph about the psychologist who developed the trait-factor theory
    D) A paragraph refuting the validity of the trait-factor theory
    E) A paragraph indicating the author's personal connection to the trait-factor theory

The correct answer is B:) A paragraph offering examples of traits that match with certain professions. Answer A is incorrect because this is the subject of the entire passage. Answer D is incorrect because the passage is describing the uses of the theory, not its insufficiencies. Answer E is incorrect because the passage is informative, not personal.

25. Which of the following would make the best thesis for the passage?

  A) The trait-factor theory is helpful in matching people with careers based on their personalities.
  B) The trait-factor theory states that writers should be creative, kind, and energetic people.
  C) The trait-factor theory is an outdated personality model.
  D) The trait-factor theory is a simple and popular job-search ideology.
  E) The paragraph should not have a thesis.

The correct answer is A:) The trait-factor theory is helpful in matching people with careers based on their personalities. This option captures the gist of what the passage is saying. That is the purpose of a thesis statement.

26. Which of the following changes should be made to line 10?

  A) Change "Therefore" to "Furthermore"
  B) Insert a semicolon after "traits"
  C) Change "successful" to "more successful"
  D) Change "choses" to "chooses"
  E) Omit "path"

The correct answer is C:) Change "successful" to "more successful." A comparison is being made so the connective "more" needs to be used.

27. Which of the following is a simple sentence?

  A) Line 10
  B) Line 7
  C) Line 9
  D) Line 5
  E) None of the above

The correct answer is D:) Line 5. Line 5 contains a single, independent clause (i.e., a single subject and verb). Therefore, it is a simple sentence.

28. The passage is written from which point of view?

   A) First person
   B) Subjunctive mood
   C) Second person singular
   D) First person plural
   E) Third person

The correct answer is E:) Third person. The passage uses all third-person references as opposed to first-person ("I") or second person ("you").

Questions 28-35 are based on the following passage:

(1) This week I decided to try out some of the new restaurants that have been opening up near my home. (2) I selected three different styles of restaurants that I wanted to try – one Chinese, one Spanish, and an Italian. (3) Each restaurant had unique and delicious food.
(4) The Chinese restaurant was nearest to the house – it was only one block away. (5) It had traditional Chinese food, such as rice and noodle dishes. (6) The restaurant also featured a unique desert called deep-fried mantou. (7) This dish is a particular favorite of the restaurant's regulars. (8) It is a platter of steamed buns served with sweetened-condensed milk.
(9) Perhaps you don't like Chinese food, though. (10) You should try the Spanish restaurant that opened up a short two blocks from my house. (11) Although there are many great dishes on the menu, you should absolutely try the Red Pine Stew. (12) This is a red bean stew with pine nuts, pancetta, chorizo, and lentils. (13) You will love it.
(14) The farthest restaurant from my home which I tried was the Italian restaurant. (15) Of the three restaurants, I must admit that this is my favorite. (16) Not only are the breadsticks fantastic and the spaghetti delicious, but also the restaurant has a traditional pasta recipe that has been passed down for generations.
(17) Trying these news restaurants has been a fun and enlightening experience. (18) It has opened me up to the many different cultures of food right here in my area. (19) I fully intend to continue in my quest, and I will try all of the restaurants near my home.

29. The passage suffers from

    A) Insufficient vocabulary
    B) Inconsistent point of view
    C) Poor punctuation
    D) Excessive clichés
    E) None of the above

The correct answer is B:) Inconsistent point of view. The first, fourth, and fifth paragraph are all written in first person. The second paragraph is written in third person. The third paragraph is written in second person.

30. This passage is written using what organizational strategy?

    A) Spatial
    B) Compare/contrast
    C) Chronological
    D) Least important to most important
    E) Both A and C

The correct answer is E:) Both A and C. The passage describes the restaurants visited in order of both location (how far from the speaker's house) and time (first to last).

31. Which of the following is a complex sentence?

    A) 1
    B) 7
    C) 13
    D) 15
    E) 19

The correct answer is E:) 19. A complex sentence has an independent and a dependent clause, as does sentence 19.

32. Which of the following is the BEST revision of line 16?

Not only are the breadsticks fantastic and the spaghetti delicious, but also the restaurant has a traditional pasta recipe that has been passed down for generations.

- A) Not only are the breadsticks fantastic and the spaghetti delicious, but also the restaurant has a traditional pasta recipe that has been passed down for generations.
- B) Not only are the breadsticks and spaghetti fantastic, but the restaurant also has a traditional pasta recipe that has been passed down for generations.
- C) Not only is the breadsticks and spaghetti fantastic and delicious, but also the restaurant features a particularly traditional pasta recipe that hast been past down for generations.
- D) The traditional pasta recipe is great.
- E) The breadsticks, spaghetti, and pasta are very yummy.

The correct answer is B:) Not only are the breadsticks and spaghetti fantastic, but the restaurants also has a traditional pasta recipe that has been passed down for generations. Answer A can be eliminated because "also" should be placed before "has." Answer C is incorrect because "past" is incorrectly used instead of "passed." Answers D and E can be eliminated because they do not contain all of the information.

33. Line 2 lacks which of the following?

- A) Parallelism; "an Italian" should be changed to "one Italian"
- B) Rhetorical emphasis; "most importantly" should be added before "an Italian"
- C) First-person point of view; it should read "you wanted to try"
- D) Punctuation; the commas should all be changed to colons
- E) A subject; "I selected" should be "Me and you selected"

The correct answer is A:) Parallelism; "an Italian" should be changed to "one Italian." This is necessary in order for the line to be parallel.

34. Which of the following additions to paragraph 3 would be most appropriate?

    A) All of the ingredients are grown from scratch, so all of the dishes have a nice, fresh flavor.
    B) It would be a good idea to go there only if you enjoy Chinese food.
    C) If you like Italian food, you will definitely like this restaurant.
    D) I was very pleased with the food selection, and would go back any day.
    E) The Spanish restaurant makes fresh flour tortillas every day.

The correct answer is A:) All of the ingredients are grown from scratch, so all of the dishes have a nice, fresh flavor. Answer B is not correct because the paragraph is promoting the food, not recommending it conditionally. Answer C is wrong because the third paragraph is not about Italian food. Answer D is wrong because the rest of the paragraph is written in second person. Answer E is incorrect because the paragraph is not about the Spanish restaurant.

35. The following line should be added to which paragraph?

Although pancetta is not a traditional Chinese ingredient, it is a fabulous addition to the stew.

    A) Paragraph 1
    B) Paragraph 2
    C) Paragraph 3
    D) Paragraph 4
    E) Paragraph 5

The correct answer is C:) Paragraph 3. This is the paragraph about the Chinese restaurant, so it would make the most sense in this paragraph.

Questions 36-43 are based on the following passage:

(1) A metropolitan area, or metropolis, is basically a large city. (2) A metropolis includes the main city and any surrounding suburban areas. (3) Generally, a metropolis has at least 50,000 people in the main city with more in the surrounding areas. (4) Tokyo is considered the largest metropolitan area in the world. (5) A megalopolis forms when two or more metropolitan areas grow so large that their boundaries begin to overlap. (6) A megalopolis is characterized by dense population, high levels of urbanization, and they always have a thriving economy.
(7) In the United States there are a number of important megalopolis regions. (8) For example, one important west-coast megalopolis is referred to as the Northern California megalopolis. (9) This megalopolis comprises the major cities of Fresno, Reno, Sacramento, San Francisco, and others in the surrounding area.
(10) The largest megalopolis areas in the country, however, are found farther east. (11) One of the most famous megalopolis areas in the United States was referred to as the Northeast megalopolis, or more simply as BosNyWash. (12) This megalopolis spans the three major cities of Boston, New York, and Washington DC. (13) It is also comprised of the major cities of Baltimore, Philadelphia, Hartford, and others.

36. The following sentence would fit most logically in which paragraph?

Paris and New York are both examples of metropolitan areas.

A) Paragraph 1
B) Paragraph 2
C) Paragraph 3
D) It should be its own paragraph after paragraph 3
E) It should be its own paragraph before paragraph 1

The correct answer is A:) Paragraph 1. The remainder of the passage is describing various megalopolis areas. Only the first paragraph talks about metropolitan areas, so it would most logically fit there.

37. Which of the following corrections must be made?

A) Change the comma before "however" in line 10 to a semicolon
B) Omit the comma after "Generally" in line 2
C) Insert a comma after "by" in line 6
D) Change the comma after "megalopolis" in line 11 to a colon
E) None of the above

The correct answer is B:) Omit the comma after "Generally" in line 2. Because Generally is an adverb, no comma is necessary.

38. The passage is written in

    A) First person plural
    B) First person singular
    C) Second person
    D) Spanish persuasive style
    E) Third person

The correct answer is E:) Third person. If it were written it third person the passage would contain the words "I" or "we." If it were written in the second person it would use "you." Therefore, it must be written in the third person. Furthermore, most academic writing is in the third person.

39. "It" in line 13 refers to

    A) Tokyo
    B) Northern California megalopolis
    C) BosNyWash
    D) Washington DC
    E) Metropolises

The correct answer is C:) BosNyWash. The line is describing additional information about this particular megalopolis.

40. Which of the following would make the most appropriate title for the passage?

    A) All About BosNyWash
    B) European Urban Centers
    C) Political Corruption Leads to Urbanization
    D) The Major Cities of Northern California
    E) North American Megalopolises

The correct answer is E:) North American Megalopolises. Answer A is wrong because the passage is about more than just the megalopolis of BosNyWash. Answer B is wrong because the passage hardly mentions European cities. Answer C is not even mentioned in the passage, and answer D is wrong because cities other than those in California are discussed.

41. Which line does NOT have parallel structure?

    A) Line 1
    B) Line 6
    C) Line 8
    D) Line 10
    E) Line 11

The correct answer is B:) Line 6. The phrase "and they have a high level of urbanization" is not parallel with the other elements listed.

42. Which of the following revisions must be made to line 11?

    A) Change "areas" to "area"
    B) Omit "in the United States"
    C) Insert a comma after "areas"
    D) Change "was referred to" to "is referred to"
    E) None of the above

The correct answer is D:) Change "was referred to" to "is referred to." Facts that are still true should always be referred to in the present tense.

43. Which of the following details would most improve paragraph 3?

    A) A metropolitan area is smaller than a megalopolis area.
    B) Many popular megalopolis regions also exist in Western Europe.
    C) The BosNyWash area supports a population of well over 50 million people.
    D) A megalopolis, such as BosNyWash, is a large urban center.
    E) None of the above could be logically used in paragraph 3.

The correct answer is C:) The BosNyWash area supports a population of well over 50 million people. The third paragraph provides information about this particular metropolitan area, so answers A and B can be eliminated. Answer D can be eliminated because the information is redundant. Answer C is the correct answer because it would add relevant information to the passage.

Questions 44-50 are based on the following passage:

(1) The story of a woman who left her family in search of self-fulfillment wouldn't be given a second thought in today's world. (2) As women, you have the right to vote. (3) But almost a hundred years ago, society was shocked by the story of Edna Pontellier, the charming, intelligence, beautiful woman who left her successful, devoted husband and two children in search of some elusive happiness. (4) *The Awakening* by Kate Chopin, published in 1899, created a controversy by dealing with subjects thought to be "sacred." (5) As Larger Ziff says in his book, *The American 1890's,* Chopin's novel was censored because it "rejected the family as the automatic equivalent of feminine self-fulfillment." (6) The novel has been interpreted as an early feminist work, as a purely sexual "awakening" in the life of a woman, as the ultimate quest for self-fulfillment, and as the Naturalistic statement on life. (7) In truth, however, no single theme is dominant. (8) *The Awakening* integrates all of these elements into a central plot with the real message being that without self-sacrifice there is no true happiness and no true love.

44. In the fourth sentence, the writer uses the word "sacred" to mean

    A) intensely spiritual
    B) exotic and mysterious
    C) religious, ritualized
    D) set apart from use; taboo
    E) frightening

The correct answer is D:) set apart from use; taboo. Although all of the answer choices are correct interpretations of the word "sacred," in the particular context of the sentence it is being used to indicate that something is considered 'off-limits' as a subject of writing. Therefore, the correct answer is D.

45. Which of the following choices is NOT true about the phrase "As Larger Ziff says…" found in line 5?

    A) the author agrees with another writer
    B) the author disagrees with another writer
    C) the author is giving credit to another writer's ideas
    D) the author is using another writer's ideas to prove her point
    E) the author is paraphrasing another writer

The correct answer is B:) the author disagrees with another writer. The author clear agrees with the passage that is quoted, and uses it to support the ideas presented in the passage.

46. The phrase "rejected the family as the automatic equivalent of feminine self-fulfill-ment" could be more simply phrased as

    A) Family equals self
    B) Having no family automatically made a woman unhappy
    C) Family problems create selfish women
    D) Female self-fulfillment occurs automatically with a family
    E) Having a family does not automatically fulfill a woman

The correct answer is E:) Having a family does not automatically fulfill a woman. Answers A, B, and D can be eliminated because they phrase the exact opposite of what the line is indicating. Answer C can be eliminated because the passage does not present women as selfish. This leaves answer E as correct.

47. The main thesis of the passage is

    A) *The Awakening* is an early Feminist work
    B) *The Awakening* is about sexual awakenings
    C) *The Awakening* is about the quest for self-fulfillment
    D) *The Awakening* is about nature and its connection to life
    E) *The Awakening* is about the effect of self-sacrifice on happiness and love

The correct answer is E:) *The Awakening* is about the effect of self-sacrifice on happiness and love. This is stated in the concluding line of the sentence. As a result, the final line essentially acts as the thesis for the passage.

48. Which line should be eliminated?

    A) Line 2
    B) Line 4
    C) Line 5
    D) Line 7
    E) Line 8

The correct answer is A:) Line 2. This line is irrelevant to the rest of the passage. It is not referring to the book, or to any of the topics the book is meant to address.

49. Which of the following is an example of parallelism?

   A) "who left her family in search" (line 1)
   B) "integrates all of these elements" (line 7)
   C) "the automatic equivalent of feminine self-fulfillment" (line 5)
   D) "no true happiness and no true love" (line 8)
   E) "and as the Naturalistic statement on life" (line 6)

The correct answer is D:) "no true happiness and no true love" (line 8). This phrase demonstrates parallelism by repeating the phrase "no true" before each characteristic.

50. Which line is NOT written from the same point-of-view as the others?

   A) Line 2
   B) Line 4
   C) Line 5
   D) Line 6
   E) Line 7

The correct answer is A:) Line 2. Line two is written in second person, which is not used in the remainder of the passage.

Questions 51-57 are based on the following passage:

(1) An oligopoly is a type of market which is characterized by the dominance of a few large companies. (2) Unlike a pure competition market, in which companies operate relatively independent of each other, the companies in an oligopoly are largely aware of one another's actions. (3) In addition to monitoring each other's actions they use strategy to determine their own moves and predict the moves of others.

(4) One type of game theory, and the most popular, is the Prisoner's Dilemma. (5) Imagine that two criminals are arrested for committing a crime. (6) They are split up and questioned separately. (7) If neither of them confess, it is likely that they will only go to jail for a short amount of time, maybe three years, due to lack of strong evidence. (8) They are both offered a deal. (9) If they confess they will get a shorter term of one year, while their partner goes to jail for a long time, ten years. (10) This makes the optimal strategy for both to confess, and only receive one year. (11) However not knowing what their partner will do or say under pressure leaves them with a tough decision.

51. Where would it make the most sense to add the following lines to the essay?

Game theory is an important aspect of oligopolies. It focuses on the reactions of members of a group in different situations.

    A) After the second paragraph
    B) After the first paragraph
    C) After line 4
    D) Before line 1
    E) After line 2

The correct answer is B:) After the first paragraph. Game theory is discussed in the second paragraph; therefore, it is most logical to place it here and introduce the topic.

52. In context, which of the following is the best replacement for the word "strong" in line 7?

    A) Convincing
    B) Muscular
    C) Legitimate
    D) Powerful
    E) Defining

The correct answer is A:) Convincing. Although all of the answers are possible interpretations of the word strong. However, in the context of evidence the most logical interpretation is convincing.

53. Which of the following is the best revision of line 10?

    A) This makes the optimal strategy for both to confess, and only receive one
       year.
    B) This means it is smartest for them to only receive one year, and confess.
    C) This means the optimal strategy is to only receive one year.
    D) This means that they both should confess, and only receive one year,
       because it is the optimal strategy.
    E) This means that the optimal strategy is for both of the criminals to confess
       because they will each receive only one year.

The correct answer is E:) This means that the optimal strategy is for both of the criminals to confess because they will each receive only one year. Answers A, B, and C all
have the misplaced modifier "only." Answer D is less concise than E.

54. Which of the following changes MUST be made to line 11?

    A) Insert a comma after "pressure"
    B) Eliminate the word "tough"
    C) Insert a comma after "However"
    D) Change "leaves" to "leafs"
    E) Change "partner" to "spouse"

The correct answer is C:) Insert a comma after "However." However is an introductory
element in the sentence, and must be offset with a comma.

55. In context, what is the best way to combine lines 5 and 6?

    A) Imagine that two criminals are arrested for committing a crime; they are
       split up and questioned separately.
    B) Imagine that two criminals are arrested for committing a crime, and they are
       split up and questioned separately.
    C) Imagine that two criminals are arrested for committing a crime, but they are
       split up and questioned separately.
    D) Two criminals are split up and questioned separately after imagining that
       they are arrested for committing a crime.
    E) Imagine that two criminals, after they are split up and questioned separately,
       are arrested for committing a crime.

The correct answer is C:) Imagine that two criminals are arrested for committing a
crime, but they are split up and questioned separately. This option correctly uses the
past-tense form of "arrest" and uses a comma and coordinating conjunction to separate
the two clauses.

56. Where would it make the most sense to place a comma in line 3?

    A) After "addition"
    B) After "monitoring"
    C) After "own moves"
    D) After "actions"
    E) After "determine"

The correct answer is D:) After "actions." "In addition to monitoring each other's actions" is an introductory element to the sentence. Therefore, it requires a comma to offset if from the rest of the sentence.

57. Which of the following best describes the main idea of the essay?

    A) To discuss the difference between pure competition markets and oligopolies.
    B) To inform the reader of the existence of oligopolies in today's world.
    C) To convince the reader that the best strategy when confronted with a Prisoner's Dilemma situation is to confess immediately.
    D) To discuss what oligopolies are, and what game theory is.
    E) To analyze the effect of oligopolies on the world economy.

The correct answer is D:) To discuss what oligopolies are, and what game theory is. The passage has two paragraphs. The first discusses oligopolies, and the second discusses game theory. Therefore, the most correct option is the one that identifies both.

Questions 58-62 are based on the following passage:

(1) The truth is most people are a combination of their met programs and internal and external frames. (2) However, if a child becomes too externally framed, they will be influenced by whatever the crowd is doing. (3) The problem with this type of thinking is the average person in the crowd is barely paying their bills and certainly not a success. (4) If Thomas Edison was an external thinker do you think he would have discovered the light bulb? (5) If John F. Kennedy was externally framed, do you think he would have ordered a military blockade against Cuba. (6) Or do you think he would have listened to Kruschev and allowed Soviet nuclear sites to be permanently established 90 miles away from Florida Keys.

58. Which is the best way to rewrite line 1 to make it less awkward and to clarify its meaning?

    A) Most people are a combination of their inherited behaviors and internal and external frames.
    B) The truth is that most people are a combination of their met behaviors and internal and external frames.
    C) The truth is most people are a combination of their met behaviors and internal and external thoughts.
    D) Most people are a combination of their met programs and internal and external frames.
    E) The truth is most people are a combination of their inherited behaviors and internal and external frames.

The correct answer is A:) Most people are a combination of their inherited behaviors and internal and external frames. This option is concise, and still contains all of the necessary information of the sentence.

59. Which is the best way to combine lines 1 and 2?

A) The truth is most people are a combination of their met programs and internal and external frames; however, if a child becomes too externally framed, they will be influenced by what the crowd is doing.

B) The truth is most people are a combination of their met programs and internal and external frames and if a child becomes too externally framed, they will be influenced by what the crowd is doing.

C) The truth is most people are a combination of their met programs and internal and external frames, in fact if a child becomes too externally framed, they will be influenced by what the crowd is doing.

D) The truth is most people are a combination of their met programs and internal and external frames; although if a child becomes too externally framed, they will be influenced by what the crowd is doing.

E) The truth is most people are a combination of their met programs and internal and external frames thus if a child becomes too externally framed they will be influenced by what the crowd is doing.

The correct answer is A:) The truth is most people are a combination of their met programs and internal and external frames; however, if a child becomes too externally framed, they will be influenced by what the crowd is doing. This option correctly uses the semicolon to combine the two sentences.

60. What is the best rewrite of line 2?

A) However, if children become too externally framed, the crowd will influence what he/she is doing.

B) However, if a child becomes too externally framed, he/she will be influenced by whatever the crowd is doing.

C) However, if a child becomes too externally framed, the crowd will influence what they are doing.

D) However, if the children become too externally framed, he/she will be influenced by whatever the crowd is doing.

E) However, if children become too externally framed, they will be influenced by whatever the crowd is doing.

The correct answer is E:) However, if children become too externally framed, they will be influenced by whatever the crowd is doing. This is the only option with the correct matching of references and pronouns.

61. What is the best rewrite of the underlined portion of line 3 (reproduced below)?

The problem with this type of <u>thinking is the average person in the crowd is barely paying their bills</u> and certainly not a success.

    A) thinking is that average people are barely paying their bills
    B) thinking is the average person in the crowd is barely paying his/her bills
    C) thinking is the average person in the crowd are barely paying their bills
    D) thinking is that the average person in the crowd is barely paying their bills
    E) thinking is that the average people in the crowd are barely paying his/her bills

The correct answer is A:) thinking is that average people are barely paying their bills. This option is the only which has the correct matchup of pronouns and verb forms.

62. What is the best rewrite of the underlined portion of line 4 (reproduced below)?

<u>If Thomas Edison was an external thinker</u> do you think he would have discovered the light bulb?

    A) If Thomas Edison was an external thinker
    B) If Thomas Edison is an external thinker
    C) If Thomas Edison had been an external thinker
    D) If Thomas Edison could be an external thinker
    E) If Thomas Edison might have been an external thinker

The correct answer is C:) If Thomas Edison had been an external thinker. Thomas Edison lived in the past, therefore the reference to him must be past tense. The most logical answer is option C.

Questions 63-69 are based on the following passage:

(1) Charles Henry is a successful general contractor who has built 47 communities in the southeast. (2) He remembers good times with his father building a clubhouse and a tree house in his back yard, where all the kids on the block used to play. (3) His father put him on the payroll when he was 11, and working on the weekends he earned enough money to pay for college. (4) However, after 3 years in college his father took ill, and he dropped out and helped him run the business. (5) He had so much enjoyment running the business he decided to earn his own general contractor license and is now Vice President of the company. (6) He says that even though many of his close friends are smarter and had better grades than him, most of them are struggling to find decent jobs.

63. Which of the following statements best describes the relationship of line 1 to the rest of the paragraph?

    A) It is the topic sentence; in other words, it establishes the organization of the paragraph as a whole.
    B) It is just the first sentence of several about the writer's background.
    C) It is not important to the paragraph as a whole.
    D) It could be left out without damaging the paragraph.
    E) It is an introductory sentence but not the topic sentence.

The correct answer is A:) It is the topic sentence; in other words, it establishes the organization of the paragraph as a whole. The passage is about Charles Henry, and how he got to be who he is. Therefore, the sentence which introduces him, as the first line does, is the topic sentence.

64. The following line would be most logically inserted where in the paragraph?

Although he was not the smartest of his friends, he did well in college and enjoyed learning.

    A) At the end of line 1
    B) At the beginning of line 3
    C) After line 3
    D) At the beginning of line 5
    E) After line 6

The correct answer is C:) After line 3. Line 3 introduces the idea of going to college, and line four speaks of him leaving college. Therefore, the actual reference to college makes the most sense between these two lines.

65. Which of the following statements best describes the relationship of line 6 to the rest of the paragraph?

    A) It is the topic sentence; in other words, it is the organizing idea of the paragraph.
    B) As the closing sentence, it completes the idea introduced in line 1.
    C) It is just another detail about the contractor's background.
    D) It is not essential to the meaning of the paragraph.
    E) It is just extra information and doesn't play an important role in the paragraph.

The correct answer is B:) As the closing sentence, it completes the idea introduced in line 1. Line 6 is the final sentence of the passage. This makes it the conclusion.

66. Which of the following revisions must be made to the paragraph?

    A) Change "47" in line 1 to "forty-seven"
    B) Change "11" in line 3" to "eleven"
    C) Change "tree house" in line 2 to "tree-house"
    D) Change "3" in line 4 to "three"
    E) Omit line 6 entirely

The correct answer is D:) Change "3" in line 4 to "three." Numbers less than ten should always be written in letter form.

67. Which of the following statements best describes the relationship of sentence 2 to the rest of the paragraph?

    A) It is the second part of a two-part topic sentence.
    B) It gives background detail that makes a bridge between the topic sentence (2) and the concluding sentence (6).
    C) It is just extra information and doesn't play an important role in the paragraph.
    D) Its purpose is to involve the reader emotionally.
    E) It begins a narrative sequence that leads from the topic sentence to the conclusion.

The correct answer is E:) It begins a narrative sequence that leads from the topic sentence to the conclusion. The lines in question give the narrative, or story, of the subject's life. Therefore, this is the most correct description of them.

68. Which of the following statements best describes the relationship of lines 3-5 to the rest of the paragraph?

    A) They provide a narrative bridge between the topic sentence and the concluding sentence.
    B) They merely provide unimportant background information, and could easily be omitted.
    C) Together, they make up the topic sentence.
    D) Their purpose is to involve the reader emotionally.
    E) They are interesting but not important to the paragraph.

The correct answer is A:) They provide a narrative bridge between the topic sentence and the concluding sentence. The lines in question give the narrative, or story, of the subject's life. Therefore, this is the most correct description.

69. Which of the following statements best describes the relationship of sentence 5 to the rest of the paragraph?

    A) It is the conclusion
    B) It introduces sentence 6, which is the conclusion
    C) It restates the topic sentence
    D) It is the topic sentence
    E) It concludes the narrative sequences and leads to the conclusion

The correct answer is E:) It concludes the narrative sequence and leads to the conclusion. Line 5 is the second to last line. It is the final line of the body of the passage, and precedes the concluding line. Therefore, this is the most correct description of it.

Questions 70-77 are based on the following passage:

(1) It was the day of six-year-old Tommy's first baseball game and he couldn't wait to wake up that morning. (2) He was out of bed at the crack of dawn and began finding himself something to eat for breakfast. (3) His team had spent alot of time practising, over the past three week, and he was sure that they would win. (4) He went to the cereal cupboard and pulled out his favorite cereal. (5) Then, he went to the fridge to get some milk. (6) It was at this point that he ran into a problem: he wasn't tall enough to reach the bowls. (7) After considering his quandary for a moment, he went around the counter and pulled over a stool. (8) He ate proudly his breakfast.

(9) With his breakfast finished, Tommy returned to his room and began looking for his uniform. (10) He went through every drawer and pulled out every piece of clothing. (11) There was no uniform. (12) He searched under his bed, in his toy chest and In his closet. (13) Still, though, he could not find his uniform. (14) As a last resort, Tommy ran down the hall and into the laundry room, dumping out every basket of clothing until he finally found it.

(15) Tommy dressed quickly and gathered up his equipment. (16) Certain that it would be time to leave soon, he started practicing his swing and imagined himself making a home run. (17) Then, his mother walked into his room and surprised him by exclaiming "What are you doing? It's two o'clock in the morning!"

70. Which of the following would best replace the word "quandary" in line 7?

   A) Dilemma
   B) Breakfast
   C) Choices
   D) Position
   E) Surroundings

The correct answer is A:) Dilemma. This is the definition of the word quandary. Furthermore, the passage at this point is describing a problem that the subject has encountered. Therefore, this is the most logical replacement word.

71. Which of the following is NOT a revision that should be made to line 3?

    A) Change "alot" to "a lot"
    B) Change "practising" to "practicing"
    C) Remove the comma after "practising"
    D) Change "week" to "weeks"
    E) All of the above corrections should be made

The correct answer is E:) All of the above corrections should be made. The word a lot should never appear as it does in the passage. Further, practicing is spelled incorrectly, and weeks must be plural to agree with the subject.

72. Which of the following is the best revision of line 8?

    A) He ate proudly his breakfast.
    B) He ate his breakfast proudly.
    C) He, proudly, ate his breakfast.
    D) He ate his proudly breakfast.
    E) He ate, his breakfast, proudly.

The correct answer is B:) He ate his breakfast proudly. Answer A has the adverb incorrectly placed in the sentence, as does answer D. Answer C has extra commas, as does answer E. Therefore, answer B must be correct.

73. In context, which line should be eliminated from the first paragraph?

    A) Line 2
    B) Line 3
    C) Line 4
    D) Line 7
    E) Line 8

The correct answer is B:) Line 3. Although line 3 does provide additional information, the reference to his team's practice schedule is a deviation from the remainder of the paragraph which is a narrative of Tommy getting breakfast.

74. What does "it" in line 14 refer to?

   A) His bat
   B) His baseball
   C) His uniform
   D) His shoes
   E) His pajamas

The correct answer is C:) His uniform. The passage leading to this point has consisted of a description of Tommy's efforts to find his uniform. It is therefore only logical that the uniform is the antecedent of "it."

75. Which of the following best combines lines 10 and 11?

   A) He went through every drawer and pull out every piece of clothing, but he still couldn't find his uniform.
   B) He pulled every piece of clothing, opened every drawer, and couldn't find his uniform.
   C) He went through every drawer, pulled out every piece of clothing, and no uniform.
   D) There was still no uniform after he went through every draw and pulled out every piece of clothing.
   E) He went through every drawer and pulled out every piece of clothing; however, he still could not find his uniform.

The correct answer is E:) He went through every drawer and pulled out every piece of clothing; however, he still could not find his uniform. This option makes correct use of a semicolon and the conjunctive adverb "however" in combining the two sentences.

76. Line 17 is primarily used to

   A) Display a larger meaning to the story
   B) Create a sense of nostalgia in the reader
   C) Make Tommy look like a fool
   D) Show his mother's annoyance
   E) Create a comic ending

The correct answer is E:) Create a comic ending. There is no larger meaning hinted at in the story, so answer A can be eliminated. Further, the passage does not indicate any annoyance on the part of his mother, so this option can be eliminated as well.

77. Which of the following best describes the passage?

    A) An excerpt from a historical novel
    B) A children's story
    C) A passage from a scientific journal
    D) An excerpt from a famous literary work
    E) An entry in an encyclopedia

The correct answer is B:) A children's story. The simple language and childlike comedy of the story eliminate more formal publications such as answers A, C, D, and E as plausible.

Questions 78-87 are based on the following passage:

(1) The Civil War was one of the worst wars the United States has been involved in. (2) Although it was not necessarily the beginning of the war, the first battle was Fort Sumter. (3) What made it the Civil War so terrible was that every soldier killed was an American, meaning that the overall American deaths were greater than in many other wars combined. (4) The war started in 1861, but the tensions and problems that caused it were building for long before that.

(5) Slavery was one of the main issues behind the war: but it was not the direct cause. (6) What caused the first wave of states to secede, starting the war, was the election of Abraham Lincoln. (7) Not a single southern state had voted for him, yet he was to be the next president. (8) The war is considered to have begun with the secession of South Carolina, which was soon followed by the states of Mississippi, Florida, Alabama, Georgia, Louisiana and Texas. (9) These states were later joined by others, with a total of 11 states seceding and calling themselves the Confederate States of America.

(10) Fort Sumter was a military fort in South Carolina which the Confederacy ordered Lincoln to surrender to them. (11) Lincoln refused to surrender the fort and the Confederacy proceeded to bombard it. (12) Because relief did not arrive in time, they were forced to surrender and Lincoln began raising troops to take it again. (13) He got around the laws requiring him to ask Congress for a declaration of war because he refused to acknowledge the Confederacy as a sovereign state. (14) Instead, he viewed their secession as an insurrection and commenced restoring order.

(15) The four-year struggle between the North and the South changed the face of the country permanently. (16) Extensive damage had been done to areas where fighting occurred and even a new state was created (West Virginia). (17) However, the war had positive aspects as well. (18) It kept the country together, and showed the states that the

Federal government would not allow them disregard laws. (19) It also provided a way for the abolition of slavery.

78. Which of the following corrections should be made to line 3?

    A) Move it to the end of the passage
    B) Add a comma after the word "killed"
    C) Put a question mark at the end because it starts with an interrogative pronoun
    D) Remove the word "it"
    E) No change is necessary

The correct answer is D:) Remove the word "it." The pronoun is unnecessary because the Civil War is identified as well.

79. Which of the following line changes should be made to improve the flow of the essay?

    A) Move line 2 so that it is after line 9
    B) Move line 6 so that it is before line 5
    C) Move line 8 so that it is after line 6
    D) Move line 11 so that it is after line 13
    E) Move line 15 to the beginning of the passage

The correct answer is A:) Move line 2 so that it is after line 9. This best improves the flow of the passage because line 2 is referencing Fort Sumter which is not discussed until line 9.

80. Which of the following corrections should be made to line 5?

    A) Change the colon to a period
    B) Change the colon to a comma
    C) Add a comma after "but"
    D) Change issues" to "issue"
    E) Remove the word "direct"

The correct answer is B:) Change the colon to a comma. This passage uses the colon incorrectly. The comma should be used instead because it is the appropriate choice to join two independent clauses when a coordinating conjunction is present.

81. The passage is written in what tense?

    A) First person singular
    B) First person plural
    C) Second person singular
    D) Interrogative
    E) Third person

The correct answer is E:) Third person. If the passage were first person it would use "I" or "we." If it were in second person it would use "you." Interrogative is not a tense. Therefore, E must be the correct answer.

82. Which of the following would most contribute to the content of the essay as a whole?

    A) Talking less about how the war was started
    B) Checking for correct spelling and punctuation throughout
    C) Adding additional information about the major battles and the course of the war
    D) Removing all references to the Confederate States of America
    E) Using more pronoun references

The correct answer is C:) Adding additional information about the major battles and the course of the war. The content of the passage would not be affected by options B, D, or E, so each of these options can be eliminated. Further, it is not logical to talk less about how the war was started in a description of the war. Therefore, answer C is the correct answer.

83. Which of the following corrections should be made to line 8?

    A) A semicolon should be added after "by" because it is the beginning of a list.
    B) A comma should be added after "Louisiana"
    C) Only the name of the first state in the list needs to be capitalized
    D) There should not be a comma following South Carolina because it is not followed by a conjunction
    E) None of the above

The correct answer is B:) A comma should be added after "Louisiana." A comma should appear after each element in a list.

84. What change should be made to the underlined portion of line 16 (reproduced below)?

Extensive damage had been done to areas where fighting <u>occurred, and even a new state was created (West Virginia)</u>.

   A) Move "even" to after "was"
   B) Add a comma after "created"
   C) Extend the parentheses to also include "created"
   D) Do not capitalize "West Virginia"
   E) Change "occurred" to "occurs"

The correct answer is A:) Move "even" to after "was." All of the verbs are used correctly, as are the parentheses, so options C, D, and E can be eliminated. It is not necessary to place any punctuation after "created." This leaves only option A.

85. The word "they" in line 12 refers to whom?

   A) The Confederacy
   B) Lincoln
   C) The relief effort
   D) Fort Sumter
   E) The states

The correct answer is D:) Fort Sumter. The only individuals in the passage who are ordered to surrender are those in Fort Sumter. Further, the prior sentence was referencing them. Therefore, the correct answer must be D.

86. According to the passage

   A) The Civil War was directly caused by slavery
   B) The Civil War was inexpensive
   C) One of the main issues of the Civil War was slavery
   D) There was no legitimate reason for the Civil War
   E) None of the above

The correct answer is C:) One of the main issues of the Civil War was slavery. This is stated in the passage whereas the other options are either contradicted or not addressed.

87. Which of the following best describes the main focus of the passage?

   A) To discuss the major battles of the Civil War
   B) To explain why slavery was the only real cause of the Civil War
   C) To describe the events of Fort Sumter
   D) To convince the reader that it was noble of Lincoln to abolish slavery
   E) To briefly discuss some causes and effects of the Civil War

The correct answer is E:) To briefly discuss some causes and effects of the Civil War. The passage introduces the first battle of the war, and it concludes by describing the end. Therefore, this is the most accurate description of the passage.

Questions 88- 92 are based on the following passage:

(1) Strip cropping is a type of farming in which crops are planted in alternating strips, with one being the crop and the other being some sort of grass or hay. (2) The strips are then lined at a right angle against the wind, or slopes to maximize the erosion prevention. (3) Contour cropping is a type of farming in which planting is along contours instead of up and down slopes. (4) This way any excess water runs into crops farther down. (5) The two methods are most useful when practiced together in strip-contour cropping. (6) This is when the crops are planted in alternating strips which run along the contour instead of up and down a slope. (7) This helps to decrease soil erosion and makes more effective use of rainfall.

88. Which of the following would best improve the quality of the paragraph as a whole?

   A) A stronger conclusion
   B) Statistical comparing to two types of farming
   C) An introduction
   D) More specific examples
   E) Checking to make sure all words are spelled correctly

The correct answer is C:) An introduction. The passage jumps straight into a description of different types of farming without any indication of the direction that the paragraph will take. Therefore it would be greatly improved by the addition of introductory information.

89. Which of the following revisions to line 3 is most needed?

   A) Insert "specific" before the word "type"
   B) Insert "done" after "planting is"
   C) Insert a comma after "farming"
   D) Change "up and down" to "on"
   E) Move the line to later in the paragraph

The correct answer is B:) Insert "done" after "planting is." The verb planting used in this context is more logical with the word done to complete it.

90. In context, line 7 serves to

   A) Better explain why contour cropping is useful
   B) Conclude the paragraph and summarize the benefits of strip-contour cropping
   C) Introduce the next topic
   D) Offer a refutation of the preceding argument
   E) None of the above

The correct answer is B:) Conclude the paragraph and summarize the benefits of strip-contour cropping. Line 7 is the final line of the passage, so answer C can be eliminated. Also, it summarizes the passage rather than refutes it, so option D can be eliminated. This means that answer B is a correct description of line 7.

91. Which correction should be made to line 2?

   A) Change the word "maximize" to "minimize"
   B) Add a second comma after "slopes"
   C) Further explain what a right angle is
   D) Remove the comma after "wind"
   E) Move the line to the beginning of the paragraph

The correct answer is D:) Remove the comma after "wind." Commas are used to join different clauses and phrases together. Although it must be placed before coordinating conjunctions in such instances, "or" in this case is not being used as a coordinating conjunction, and does not require a comma.

92. The passage uses which organizational strategy?

    A) Chronological
    B) Most important to least important
    C) Spatial
    D) Least helpful to most helpful
    E) Best to worst

The correct answer is D:) Least helpful to most helpful. The passage begins by describing the most primitive farming systems, and moves on to describe the most useful and advantageous methods. This makes answer D the most correct description of the passage's organization.

<u>Questions 93-100 are based on the following passage:</u>

(1) On the second day, at a distance of five hundred miles from the French coast, in the midst of a violent storm, we received the following message by means of the wireless telegraph:

(2) "Arsene Lupin is on your vessel, first cabin, blonde hair, he has a wounded right fore-arm, traveling alone under name of R........"

(3) If the news had been of some other character, I have no doubt that the secret would have been carefully guarded by the telegraphic operator as well as by the officers of the vessel. (4) But it was one of those events calculated to escape from the most rigorous discretion. (5) The same day, no one knew how, the incident becomes a matter of current gossip and every passenger was aware that the famous Arsene Lupin was hiding in our midst.

(6) Arsene Lupin in our midst! (7) The irresponsible burglar whose exploits had been narrated in all the newspapers during the past few months! (8) The mysterious individual with whom Ganimard, our shrewdest detective, had been engaged in an implacable conflict amidst interesting and picturesque surroundings. (9) I was on a boat to London. (10) Arsene Lupin, the eccentric gentleman who operates only in the chateaux and salons, and who, one night, entered the residence of Baron Schormann, but emerged empty-handed, leaving, however, his card on which he had scribbled these words: "Arsene Lupin, gentleman- burglar, will return when the furniture is genuine." (11) Arsene Lupin, the man of a thousand disguises: in turn a chauffeur, detective, bookmaker, Russian physician, Spanish bull-fighter, commercial traveler, robust youth, or decrepit old man.

93. Which of the following revisions should be made to line 1?

    A) Insert a colon in place of the first comma
    B) Place "we received" in parentheses
    C) Use "towards" instead of "from"
    D) Change "five hundred miles" to "500 miles"
    E) It should be placed at the end of the passage

The correct answer is D:) Change "five hundred miles" to "500 miles." Numbers greater than ten should be in numeral form.

94. The passage is written in which tense?

    A) First person
    B) Dictational
    C) Third person
    D) Second person
    E) Interrogative

The correct answer is A:) First person. The passage is told from the perspective of the speaker, and makes use of the pronoun "I." Therefore, it must be the first person.

95. The word "the incident" in line 5 is referring to

    A) The storm
    B) The telegraph
    C) The injury of Arsene Lupin
    D) The night's dinner
    E) None of the above

The correct answer is B:) The passage does not go into much detail about Lupin's injury, and does not ever mention dinner. Furthermore, after the passage mentions the incident, it begins to discuss the gossip about Arsene Lupin, whose presence was learned of via the telegraph. Therefore, it is referring to the telegraph and the correct answer is B.

96. The following paragraph would most logically be inserted where in the passage?

At that moment, a terrible flash of lightning rent the stormy skies. The electric waves were interrupted. The remainder of the dispatch never reached us. Of the name under Arsene Lupin was concealing himself, we knew only the initial.

    A) Before paragraph 1
    B) Before paragraph 2
    C) Before paragraph 3
    D) Before paragraph 4
    E) In the middle of paragraph 4

The correct answer is C:) Before paragraph 3.

97. The underlined portion of line 5 (reproduced below) should be edited to read what?

The same day, no one knew how, the <u>incident becomes a matter</u> of current gossip and every passenger was aware that the famous Arsene Lupin was hiding in our midst.

    A) the incident becomes a matter
    B) the incidents become matters
    C) the incident became a matter
    D) the incidents became matters
    E) the incidents became a matter

The correct answer is C:) the incident became a matter. There was only one incident that the passage is describing, so it should be singular. The passage is written in the past tense, so became should be used instead of becomes.

98. Line 2 suffers from which of the following?

    A) Lack of parallelism
    B) Improper analogy
    C) Inconsistent voice
    D) Improper use of pronounce
    E) Incorrect spelling

The correct answer is A:) Lack of parallelism. The phrase "he has a wounded right forearm" is not parallel with the remainder of the description of Arsene Lupin.

99. Which line should be omitted from the fourth paragraph?

    A) Line 7
    B) Line 8
    C) Line 9
    D) Line 10
    E) Line 11

The correct answer is C:) Line 9. The remainder of the paragraph is a description of the famous criminal Arsene Lupin. Line 9 introduces irrelevant and impertinent information, and should be eliminated from the passage.

100. The word "exploits" in line 7 functions as a(n)

    A) Verb
    B) Antecedent
    C) Pronoun
    D) Adjective
    E) Noun

The correct answer is E:) Noun. It is not a verb because it is not the action being performed. It is not an antecedent or a pronoun because it is not the subject of the sentence, nor is it referred back to with a pronoun. It is not an adjective because it is not modifying any other word. Therefore, it must be a noun.

Questions 101-107 are based on the following passage:

(1) Soon after I had thus gained a complete victory over my two powerful adversaries, my companion arrived in search of me; for finding I did not follow he into the woods, he returned, apprehending I had lost my way, or met with some accident.

(2) After mutual congratulations, we measured the crocodile, which was just forty feet in length.

(3) As soon as we had related this extraordinary adventure to the governor, he sent a wagon and servants, who brought home the two carcasses. (4) The lion's skin was properly preserved, with its hair on, after which it was made into tobacco-pouches, and presented by me, upon our return to Holland, to the burgomasters, who, in return, requested my acceptance of a thousand ducats.

(5) The skin of the crocodile was stuffed in the usual manner, and makes a capital article in their public museum at Amsterdam, where the exhibitor relates the whole story to each spectator, with such additions as he thinks properly…

(6) The little regard which this impudent knave has to veracity makes me sometimes apprehensive that my real facts may fall under suspicion, by being found in company with his confounded inventions.

101. The two powerful adversaries referenced in line 1 are

   A) Two poachers who the speaker stopped in the act of poaching
   B) Two friends with whom the speaker was involved in a game of bridge
   C) A lion and a crocodile
   D) Two lions that the speaker had been hunting all day
   E) Two crocodiles who had attacked the speaker as he stopped for a rest

The correct answer is C:) A lion and a crocodile. The passage continues on after line 1 to describe how the speaker and his friend treat a lion and a crocodile which the speaker has obtained. Therefore, it is most likely that these are the adversaries that it is referencing.

102. The word "capital" as used in line 6 means

    A) Uppercase
    B) Metropolis
    C) Distinct
    D) Monetary
    E) Excellent

The correct answer is E:) Excellent. The word capital is being used to describe the display. This means that answers A-D can be eliminated because none of them would be used to describe a display. Therefore, the correct answer is E, excellent.

103. Which of the following words is used incorrectly in the passage?

    A) "capital" in line 6
    B) "where" in line 5
    C) "acceptance" in line 4
    D) "it's" in line 4
    E) "who" in line 3

The correct answer is D:) "it's" in line 4. The word "it's" is only used as the contraction for "it is." This is not how it is being used in line 4; therefore, it is being used incorrectly.

104. Which of the following revisions must be made to line 5?

    A) Change "article" to "articles"
    B) Change "properly" to "proper"
    C) Change "where" to "were"
    D) Change "relates" to "related"
    E) "Change "their" to "they're"

The correct answer is B:) Change "properly" to "proper." Properly is an adverb, which is not the correct usage in the context of the sentence.

105. The passage would be most improved by

   A) The addition of background information about the speaker and situation.
   B) The addition of more specific measurements of the crocodile and lion.
   C) The omission of the description of the exhibitor.
   D) Being written in the interrogative form instead.
   E) More careful organization of the final two paragraphs.

The correct answer is A:) The addition of background information about the speaker and situation. The passage jumps right to a description of the results of some event, without ever introducing it. Therefore, background information would be relevant and useful in this passage.

106. Which of the following revisions of the underlined portion of line 1 (reproduced below) is correct?

Soon after I had thus gained a complete victory over my two powerful adversaries, my companion arrived in search of me; <u>for finding I did not follow he into the woods</u>, he returned, apprehending I had lost my way, or met with some accident.

   A) for finding I did not follow he into the woods
   B) for finding I do not follow he into the woods
   C) for found I did not follow him into the woods
   D) for finding I did not follow him into the woods
   E) for finding I do not follow him into the woods

The correct answer is D:) for finding I did not follow him into the woods. This option correctly uses the objective reference "him" instead of the subjective reference "he."

107. The passage most closely uses which type of organization?

   A) Compare/contrast
   B) Most important to least important
   C) Spatial
   D) Demonstrative
   E) Chronological

The correct answer is E:) Chronological. The passage is a narrative, and tells the story as it progressed. Therefore, the organization is chronological.

Questions 108-114 are based on the following passage:

(1) One of a series of scandals that occurred in France in the late 19th century was the Dreyfus Affair. (2) In 1894 Captain Alfred Dreyfus was convicted of treason for supplying the Germans with information. (3) However, he was never allowed to examine or refute the evidence against him and maintained that he was innocent. (4) It was uncovered two years later that the traitor had been another army major, and that much of the evidence against Dreyfus was in fact forged. (5) However, the army was more concerned with preserving it's reputation then righting any wrongs, and decided to pardon the guilty major and cover up their mistake. (6) Information about the cover up then spread due to the book J'accuse, written by Emile Zola, which was meant to criticize both the cover up and general corruption of the government.

108. Which of the following statements best summarizes the Dreyfus Affair as described in the passage?

    A) It was discovered that Captain Dreyfus had been involved in altering communications with French allies in an effort to prolong the war.
    B) German officer Alfred Dreyfus was discovered to have been falsely accused of murder, but was sentenced to death anyways.
    C) French Captain Dreyfus was falsely accused of giving information to the Germans on a basis of forged evidence and wrongful trial proceedings.
    D) Captain Dreyfus was discovered to have Soviet sympathies and was relieved of his post during World War II.
    E) None of the above

The correct answer is C:) French Captain Dreyfus was falsely accused of giving information to the Germans on a basis of forged evidence and wrongful trial proceedings. This option offers the best summary of the passage.

109. Which of the following revisions of the underlined portion of line 5 (reproduced below) is correct?

    However, the army was more concerned with <u>preserving it's reputation then righting</u> any wrongs, and decided to pardon the guilty major and cover up their mistake.

    A) preserving its reputation then righting
    B) preserving its reputation than righting
    C) preserving its' reputation than writing
    D) preserving it's reputation then righting
    E) preserving it's reputation than righting

The correct answer is B:) preserving its reputation than righting. This option is the only one to use the correct form of "its," "than," and "righting."

110. Line 6 suffers from

    A) Improper noun references
    B) Incorrect verb usage
    C) Lack of parallelism
    D) Irrelevance
    E) Insufficient use of pronouns

The correct answer is C:) Lack of parallelism. The phrase "general corruption" should appear "the general corruption" in order to be parallel.

111. The passage is written using which point of view?

    A) Demonstrative
    B) Interrogative
    C) Future perfect
    D) Third person
    E) Second person

The correct answer is D:) Third person. Demonstrative, interrogative, and future perfect are not points of view, so answers A, B, and C can be eliminated. If the passage were written in second person it would contain the reference you, so answer E can also be eliminated.

112. The purpose of the passage is to

    A) Inform the reader about a historical event.
    B) Present a unique perspective on government actions.
    C) Confuse the reader as to the author's opinion.
    D) Demonstrate the author's fluency in English.
    E) Engage the reader emotionally in the events of the past.

The correct answer is A:) Inform the reader about a historical event. The passage can best be described as a summary of the Dreyfus affair, making this the most logical interpretation of its purpose.

113. Which of the following is an example of a verb in the past-perfect tense?

    A) "was convicted" in line 1
    B) "then spread" in line 6
    C) "preserving" in line 5
    D) "had been" in line 4
    E) "refute" in line 3

The correct answer is D:) "had been" in line 4. The past-perfect tense is used to describe something which occurred in the past. In other words, it describes something which "passed in the past." It combines the helping verb "had" with the past tense form of the verb.

114. Which of the following lines incorrectly uses a plural reference?

    A) Line 5
    B) Line 4
    C) Line 3
    D) Line 2
    E) Line 1

The correct answer is A:) Line 5. "The army" is a singular reference, and should not be referred to with the plural reference "their" at the end of the line.

Questions 115-120 are based on the following passage:

(1) Ethan Frome is a novel by Edith Wharton. (2) The book tells the story of Ethan frome who had been injured in a "smash up," some years previously. (3) A flashback describes the story of Frome falling in love with his wife's cousin Mattie (who reciprocates his affections) who has come to care for her when she falls ill. (4) When his wife Zeena discovers this she intends to have Mattie sent away. (5) Frome and Mattie form a suicide pact, but instead the two are just permanently injured. (6) The book ends ironically, with Zeena caring for Frome and Mattie.

115. Which of the following corrections should be made to line 1?

   A) Italicize "Ethan Frome"
   B) Underline "Edith Wharton"
   C) Change "novel" to "work of fiction"
   D) Add a comma after novel
   E) Move it to the end of the paragraph

The correct answer is A:) Italicize "Ethan Frome." Ethan Frome is the title of a book and should therefore be italicized.

116. Which of the following would be the best substitute for the word "reciprocates" in line 3?

   A) Rejects
   B) Responds to
   C) Gives back
   D) Returns
   E) None of the above

The correct answer is D:) Returns. The word reciprocates indicates that Mattie is also in love with Ethan Frome, meaning that returns is the most similar in meaning.

117. Line 3 suffers from which of the following?

   A) Illogical comparative structure
   B) False logic
   C) Unclear pronoun usage
   D) Lack of parallelism
   E) Poor spelling

The correct answer is C:) Unclear pronoun usage. "She" and "her" are both referenced, making it unclear which woman is which.

118. Which of the following is a suitable revision of line 3?

    A) A flashback describes the story of Frome falling in love with his wife,
       Zeena's, cousin Mattie when she comes to care for Zeena during an illness.
    B) A flashback describes the story of Frome and his wife's cousins Mattie
       falling in love after Mattie comes to care for her when she falls ill.
    C) A flashback describes the story of Frome falling in love with his wife's
       cousin, Mattie, (who reciprocates his affections) who has come to care for
       her when she falls ill.
    D) A flashback describes the story of Frome's wife's cousin coming to care for
       his wife when she falls ill and the two of them fall in love.
    E) None of the above

The correct answer is A:) A flashback describes the story of Frome falling in love with
his wife, Zeena's, cousin Mattie when she comes to care for Zeena during an illness.
This option has clear pronoun references and correct use of the possessive form.

119. Which of the following revisions must be made to line 2?

    A) Italicize "Ethan Frome"
    B) Remove the comma after "smash up"
    C) Change the word "previously" to "formerly"
    D) "Change "had" to "has"
    E) No revisions are needed

The correct answer is B:) Remove the comma after "smash up." The comma is not necessary here because it is neither joining two clauses nor setting apart any information.

120. Which of the following best describes the main point of the paragraph?

    A) To describe the irony of the clichéd situation
    B) To convince the reader that *Ethan Frome* is a literary work
    C) To caution readers against forming suicide pacts
    D) To summarize the events of the novel *Ethan Frome*
    E) None of the above

The correct answer is D:) To summarize the events of the novel *Ethan Frome*. The
passage is a short description of the novel. Options B and C can be eliminated because
the passage neither discusses the novel's validity nor passes judgment on any of the
actions.

Questions 121-125 are based on the following passage:

(1) My older sister Melanie became the princess of my world when she bought her first prom dress, a white chiffon, high-waisted gown bordered with deep pink flowers. (2) In a little sister's devotion, I thought she was the most beautiful girl in the whole world.

(3) Melanie was my princess, then her date Tommy Nolan was my prince. (4) The high school guidance counselor let Tommy borrow his gold Cadillac to take my sister to the prom. (5) He came driving up in this freshly waxed and shining car and emerged with his arms loaded. (6) We were hardly able to see him from behind a stack of white boxes, gallantly charging up the hill to the front door.

(7) He was one of the only beaus to win my mother's heart. (8) I watched, amazed and thrilled, as he presented one of those boxes of a dozen long-stem pink roses to our mother. (9) Another box contained a dozen long-stem pink roses for Melanie. (10) In addition, there was a beautiful, fragrant bouquet topped with a white, silk butterfly for me.

(11) Melanie and Tommy departed for the ball, leaving a dewy-eyed mother, charmed little sister, and house perfumed with the scent of roses behind them.

(12) Every Spring, I think of my sister's old boyfriend and how much money had had to pay for those roses, how much thought and effort he put into making a good impression on my mom, and how well-mannered, good-natured, and gentle-hearted he always seemed.

121. Which word would best fit the beginning of line 3?

    A) Instead
    B) Consequently
    C) Moreover
    D) If
    E) So

The correct answer is D:) If. The line is not emphasizing past information, so options B and C can be eliminated. It also is not contradicting past information so option A can be eliminated. Therefore, the most fitting introductory word is if.

122. What transitional phrase provides the best paragraph link for line 7?

   A) Unbelievably, he was the one of the only beaus to win my mother's heart.
   B) Because my mother liked him, he was the only beau to win my mother's heart.
   C) On the other hand, he was one of the only beaus to win my mother's heart.
   D) No wonder he was one of the only beaus to win my mother's heart.
   E) However, he was one of the only beaus to win my mother's heart.

The correct answer is E:) However, he was one of the only beaus to win my mother's heart. Option A can be eliminated because the passage gives no indication that this is "unbelievable." Option B can be eliminated because it is redundant. Option C can be eliminated because it would make the line sound contradictory, which it is not.

123. In line 12, what grammatical structure is being utilized?

   A) Irony
   B) Metaphor
   C) Analogy
   D) Parallelism
   E) Simile

The correct answer is D:) Parallelism. The line consists of a long list of traits which are all given the same grammatical structure.

124. Which line contains an error in capitalization?

   A) Line 2
   B) Line 4
   C) Line 7
   D) Line 9
   E) Line 12

The correct answer is E:) Line 12. The word "spring" does not need to be capitalized because it is a general reference to the season, and capitalization is not necessary.

125. The word "waxed" in line 5 is a(n)

   A) Conjunction
   B) Adjective
   C) Idiom
   D) Adverb
   E) Subject

The correct answer is B:) Adjective. The word waxed is used to describe the car. Because it is being used to modify a noun it is an adjective.

Questions 126 –133 are based on the following passage:

(1) However, a depleted bank account had caused me to postpone my Holiday. (2) It was a blazing hot day in August. (3) Baker Street was like an oven, and the glare of the sunlight upon the yellow brickwork of the house across the road was painful to the eye. (4) It was hard to believe that these were the same walls which loomed so gloomily through the fogs of winter. (5) Our blinds were half-drawn, and Holmes lay curled upon the sofa, reading and re-reading a letter which he had received by the morning post. (6) For myself, my term of service in India will have trained me to stand heat better than cold, and a thermometer at ninety was no hardship. (7) But the morning paper was uninteresting. (8) Parliament had risen. (9) Everybody was out of town; and I yearned for the glades of the New Forest or the shingle of Southsea.

The Adventure of the Cardboard Box
By Sir Arthur Conan Doyle
(Altered)

126. Which line could most easily be omitted from the passage?

   A) Line 2
   B) Line 4
   C) Line 7
   D) Line 8
   E) Line 9

The correct answer is D:) Line 8. Line 8 is the least impactful line of the passage. Any of the other lines, if omitted, would detract from the lines surrounding them. However, line 8 has little to do with the other lines in the passage, and could most easily be omitted from it.

127. Line 5 is written from which point of view?

    A) First person singular
    B) First person plural
    C) Second person
    D) Third person singular
    E) Third person plural

The correct answer is B:) First person plural. The reference "our" indicates first person plural. This is because the speaker is included in the reference, but so are others.

128. Which of the following corrections should be made to line 6?

    A) Do not capitalize the word "India"
    B) Make all of the references third person
    C) Change the comma after "myself" to a semicolon
    D) Insert a comma before "hardship"
    E) Change "will have" to "had"

The correct answer is E:) Change "will have" to "had." The remainder of the sentence is written in the past tense, so this element should be as well. It would be illogical that a future event would have already trained the speaker to stand the heat.

129. Which of the following would most improve the flow of the passage?

    A) Move line 1 to the end of the passage
    B) Insert additional information about Baker street
    C) Explain further why it was so hot that August
    D) Move line 3 so that it appears after line 7
    E) Move line 6 so that it appears before line 9

The correct answer is A:) Move line 1 to the end of the passage. Line 1 makes more sense in context as a response to line 9. Therefore, it would be most logical to move this line to the end of the passage. Additionally, the word "However" is a transition and doesn't make sense without any information preceding it.

130. Which line contains a capitalization error?

    A) Line 1
    B) Line 4
    C) Line 6
    D) Line 7
    E) Line 8

The correct answer is A:) Line 1. It is not necessary to capitalize the word "Holiday" when used in this context.

131. The word "glare" as used in line 3 functions as a

    A) Verb
    B) Adjective
    C) Pronoun
    D) Noun
    E) Adverb

The correct answer is D:) Noun. The word "glare" is an object in this context; therefore, it is functioning as a noun in the sentence.

132. Which of the following revisions of line 9 is most correct?

    A) Everybody was out of town; and I yearned for the glades of the New Forest or the single of Southsea.
    B) Everybody was out of town: however, I yearned for the glades of the New Forest or the shingle of Southsea.
    C) Everybody, was out of town. However; I yearned for the glades of the New Forest or the shingle of Southsea.
    D) Everybody was out of town, although I yearned for the glades of the New Forest, or the shingle of Southsea.
    E) Everybody was out of town, and I yearned for the glades of the New Forest or the shingle of Southsea.

The correct answer is E:) Everybody was out of town, and I yearned for the glades of the New Forest or the shingle of Southsea. A semicolon is unnecessary after the word "town," so option can be eliminated. A semicolon, followed by the subordinating conjunction "however" is also incorrect, so option B can be eliminated. It is incorrect to place a semicolon after an introductory phrase, so option C can be eliminated. Option D can be eliminated because "although" does not make sense when the sentence is placed in context.

133. The passage could most correctly be described as

   A) A passage from a medical journal
   B) A narrative
   C) A store catalog
   D) A persuasive essay
   E) None of the above

The correct answer is B:) A narrative. In the passage, the speaker is describing the events of something occurring to him. Essentially he is telling a story. Therefore, a narrative is the best way to describe the passage.

Questions 134 – 140 are based on the following passage:

(1) In geography, the world can be represented in a number of different ways. (2) The two most common methods used to represent the world are a globe and a flat map. (3) Each of these methods is associated with different positive and negative aspects. (4) Globes are useful because they are the most accurate representations of the actual surface of the earth. (5) Because the earth is a sphere, the globe can show the relationships between different landmasses, oceans, and features most accurately. (6) However, globes can be disadvantageous because they are small-scale, and they are not always the most useful representations. (7) Also, because they are round it is impossible to get a whole-earth view at once, so studying large distances can be difficult. (8) Similarly, flat maps are very easy to use in judging distances, and are far more portable than globes are. (9) However, it is important to keep in mind when examining a flat map that there will be distortions in the representation of different factors because of the conversion from three dimensions to two.

134. The passage uses which type of organization?

   A) Least important to most important
   B) Chronological
   C) Compare/contrast
   D) Spatial
   E) There is no organizational pattern to this passage

The correct answer is C:) Compare/contrast. The passage compares the two different types of maps – flat maps and globes. Therefore, this is the most correct description of its organizational pattern.

135. The purpose of the passage is most likely to

    A) Confuse the reader
    B) Persuade the reader
    C) Dissuade the reader
    D) Upset the reader
    E) Inform the reader

The correct answer is E:) Inform the reader. The passage is describing the different between the two types of maps. Therefore, it is not attempting to confuse them. It also does not try to persuade the reader that one is better, so it would not make sense to claim that it is attempting to persuade the reader. The passage also does not make any emotional claims either. Therefore, the purpose of the passage is most likely to inform the reader.

136. The passage is written from which point of view?

    A) Past participle
    B) Third person
    C) Second person
    D) Progressive
    E) Diminutive

The correct answer is B:) Third person. The passage cannot be described as first person because it does not use the reference "I" or "we." It cannot be the second person because it does not use "you." Therefore, it must be written in the third person.

137. Which of the following revisions must be made to line 6?

    A) Remove the hyphen in "small-scale"
    B) Insert a comma after "disadvantageous"
    C) Remove the comma after "however"
    D) Change "most useful" to "most-useful"
    E) Change "disadvantageous" to "advantageous"

The correct answer is A:) Remove the hyphen in "small-scale." Because "small-scale" appears after the adjective, no hyphen is required in this context.

138. Which of the following is an example of a past tense verb?

    A) "associated" in line 3
    B) "can show" in line 5
    C) "there will be" in line 9
    D) "caused" in line 10
    E) "features" in line 5

The correct answer is D:) "caused" in line 10. Although it may be tempting to select "associated" in Line 3, this word is actually not used in the past tense because it has the word "is" in front of it.

139. Which of the following would make the most logical transition at the beginning of line 8?

    A) Similarly
    B) Therefore
    C) In contrast
    D) Rather
    E) In addition

The correct answer is C:) In contrast. Line 8 is the line which presents the contrasting information to the rest of the paragraph; therefore, this would be the most logical transition between the two sentences.

140. The following line would most logically be inserted where into the passage?

    This ability to represent distances accurately is the greatest strength of the globe.

    A) Before line 1
    B) After line 9
    C) After line 8
    D) Before line 3
    E) After line 5

The correct answer is E:) After line 5. Line 5 discusses the fact that distance representation is the greatest advantage of globes. This line reinforces that fact, so it is most logical to place it immediately afterwards.

Questions 141- 146 are based on the following passages:

(1) It was the first day of school, and Jen could not be more excited. (2) She had been waiting for her first day in high school all summer. (3) She liked candy canes. (4) She picked out her favorite outfit a pair of skinny jeans and a purple blouse and put it on quickly. (5) Once dressed, she hurried down the stairs for breakfast. (6) Her mom had gotten up early and made a hearty pancake breakfast, with sides of sliced fruit and bacon. (7) She enjoyed the breakfast, although she generally like sausage more then bacon.

(8) After she finished getting ready for school, Jen hopped in her car and drove to school. (9) Upon arriving, she picked up her schedule, and looked at her class list. (10) She had first English, then science, then math, then sewing, history. (11) She headed down the hallway for her English classroom. (12) It was then that she ran into the principle. (13) He asked her into his office, and invited her to be that year's school ambassador. (14) It was an extreme honor. (15) She knew then that it would be a great year.

141. Which of the following revisions of line 3 is the MOST correct?

   A) She picked out her favorite outfit a pair of skinny jeans and a purple blouse and put it on quickly.
   B) She picked out her favorite outfit – a pair of skinny jeans and a purple blouse – and put it on quickly.
   C) She picked out her favorite outfit; a pair of skinny jeans and a purple blouse; and put it on quickly.
   D) She picked out her favorite outfit – a pair of skinny jeans and a purple blouse, and put it on quickly.
   E) She picked out her favorite outfit: a pair of skinny jeans and a purple blouse; and put it on quickly.

The correct answer is B:) She picked out her favorite outfit – a pair of skinny jeans and a purple blouse – and put it on quickly. Hyphens are correctly used in this sentence to offset the additional information about the outfit.

142. Line 10 suffers from problems with which of the following?

    A) Punctuation
    B) Parallelism
    C) Chronology
    D) Analogy
    E) Pronoun usage

The correct answer is B:) Parallelism. The final element in the list "history" is not parallel with the remainder of the sentence because it does not use the word "then" as well.

143. Which of the following does NOT correctly use the word "then" correctly?

    A) Line 7
    B) Line 10
    C) Line 12
    D) Line 15
    E) All of the above use the word "then" correctly

The correct answer is A:) Line 7. This line is making a comparison, not showing chronology. Therefore, the word "than" should be used instead of "then."

144. Which of the following lines should be omitted from the first paragraph?

    A) Line 7
    B) Line 6
    C) Line 5
    D) Line 4
    E) Line 3

The correct answer is E:) Line 3. The fact that the subject, Jen, likes candy canes does not contribute to the rest of the passage. It is extra information and should be eliminated.

145. The following line would most logically be inserted where into the passage?

Since she was little she had wanted to be the school ambassador one day.

A) After line 1
B) After line 5
C) After line 9
D) After line 13
E) After line 15

The correct answer is D:) After line 13. The position of school ambassador is first mentioned in line 13, so it doesn't make sense to insert the line anywhere prior to this. Line 15 is clearly a concluding sentence, so nothing should be inserted after it.

146. Which of the following words is used incorrectly?

A) "blouse" in line 4
B) "gotten" in line 6
C) "principle" in line 12
D) "year's" in line 13
E) "great" in line 15

The correct answer is C:) "principle" in line 12. The leader of a school is the principal, not the "principle."

Questions 147- 150 are based on the following passage:

(1) Aptitude tests are analytical tests who are designed to assess the takers abilities in a variety of different areas. (2) In the field of career counseling aptitude tests are often used to gather information about a person and what their interests or skills are. (3) The individual can then be guided to appropriate jobs for their personalities. (4) Aptitude tests are also often used by organizations in screening potential employees. (5) They can be based on numeric abilities, abstract reasoning, mechanical knowledge or any other information considered important to the employer.

147. Which of the following revisions is necessary for the underlined portion of line 1 (reproduced below)?

    Aptitude tests are analytical <u>tests who are designed</u> to assess the takers abilities in a variety of different areas.

    A) tests who are designed
    B) tests who were designed
    C) tests that are designed
    D) tests that were designed
    E) tests which had been designed

The correct answer is C:) tests that are designed. The line is written in the present tense, so options B, C, and E can be eliminated. Option A can be eliminated because the word "who" is the incorrect reference for "tests."

148. Which of the following revisions should be made to Line 5?

    A) Change "reasoning" to "reasons"
    B) Change "they" to "It"
    C) Remove the commas after "abilities" and "reasoning"
    D) Insert a comma after "knowledge"
    E) None of the above

The correct answer is D:) Insert a comma after "knowledge." All of the element of a list should have commas separating them.

149. The following line should be inserted where in the passage?

Because they are used by employers, it is important that individuals are always prepared for aptitude tests, as they may make the difference in obtaining a job or promotion.

A) After line 5
B) After line 1
C) After line 3
D) Before line 1
E) After line 4

The correct answer is A:) After line 5. This line makes the most sense as a concluding line because it reinforces the information presented in line 5, and generally summarizes the passage as a whole.

150. The phrase "takers abilities in a variety of different areas" in line 1 suffers from which of the following?

A) Redundancy
B) Lack of parallelism
C) Improper use of pronounce
D) Insufficient description
E) Misplaced modifiers

The correct answer is A:) Redundancy. The adjectives "variety" and "different" both have the same meanings in context, and only one is necessary to convey the meaning of the sentence.

SECTION 3: IMPROVING PARAGRAPHS ANSWER KEY

1. C	42. D	83. B	124. E
2. B	43. C	84. A	125. B
3. E	44. D	85. D	126. D
4. A	45. B	86. C	127. B
5. D	46. E	87. E	128. E
6. E	47. E	88. C	129. A
7. B	48. A	89. B	130. A
8. C	49. D	90. B	131. D
9. B	50. A	91. D	132. E
10. E	51. B	92. D	133. B
11. C	52. A	93. D	134. C
12. E	53. E	94. A	135. E
13. A	54. C	95. B	136. B
14. B	55. C	96. C	137. A
15. E	56. D	97. C	138. D
16. D	57. D	98. A	139. C
17. A	58. A	99. C	140. E
18. B	59. A	100. E	141. B
19. C	60. E	101. C	142. B
20. B	61. A	102. E	143. A
21. C	62. C	103. D	144. E
22. E	63. A	104. B	145. D
23. D	64. C	105. A	146. C
24. B	65. B	106. D	147. C
25. A	66. D	107. E	148. D
26. C	67. E	108. C	149. A
27. D	68. A	109. B	150. A
28. E	69. E	110. C	
29. B	70. A	111. D	
30. E	71. E	112. A	
31. E	72. B	113. D	
32. B	73. B	114. A	
33. A	74. C	115. A	
34. A	75. E	116. D	
35. C	76. E	117. C	
36. A	77. B	118. A	
37. B	78. D	119. B	
38. E	79. A	120. D	
39. C	80. B	121. D	
40. E	81. E	122. E	
41. B	82. C	123. D	

Section 4: Essay

ORGANIZATION

Have you ever had a teacher tell you that your meaning was unclear, that you "rambled," or that your paragraphs were unstructured? All of these problems result from a lack of organization.

Contrary to popular opinion, the order in which ideas fall out of your head and onto the paper isn't always the best order. Most ideas need to be presented clearly in a logical progression.

Understanding the basic structure of a paragraph is essential to organization.

Some teachers want you to present a formal outline for your paper. Others will suggest that you have a written plan, perhaps less formal than a traditional outline. Still other teachers allow you to use mapping, clustering, or other graphic techniques to organize your material. The important thing is that you plan ahead of time the order of the presentation of your paper.

Some common organizational patterns are listed below:

Chronological presentation: A time-sequenced order. Evidence is presented from the oldest to the most recent. You could also work backwards, starting with the most recent evidence and working toward the first item of interest.

Least important to most important: You might want to list your details and evidence beginning with the most minor, least important points first. Each point becomes stronger and stronger until the evidence with the most weight is presented. This enables you to leave your audience with a strong final opinion that can't be refuted.

Comparison/Contrast: A strategy where you're showing how topics are similar and/or different. Basically, there are two ways to utilize this technique. First, present all the information about one topic; then present all the information about the second topic. This technique is called the "block" approach.

The second organizational pattern for comparison/contrast papers is the "point-by-point" technique. With this method, you discuss one point of the first topic and show whether it is similar or dissimilar to the second topic. Each main characteristic of a topic is discussed in comparison to the second topic, so you are skipping back and forth between topic one and topic two. This pattern is a more sophisticated pattern and more interesting to read than the simple "block" style, and many college professors prefer this strategy.

Spatial order: Another possible way to organize material is to present it in spatial order. This works particularly well for descriptive papers. Start with the details that are farthest away in your field of vision and work toward the details that are closest to you. You might also try describing the things that are closest to you and working your way to a "wide-screen" description. Either way is fine. The main issue is that you figure out a way to present your details and that you are consistent with this presentation. If you're starting with a description of something far away, then don't jump around to something nearby.

EVIDENCE

"Evidence" may be anything that helps support your point. Details, anecdotes, quotations, descriptions, statistics are all considered "evidence" if they help to make your case.

In academic writing, you must be sure to evaluate your evidence. Just because you heard it on the street or read it on the Internet, doesn't make it true. Be sure to evaluate evidence to determine its validity. Is the fact distorted by memory or time? Is there a credible source? Is the idea logical?

Once you get to the college level, you are not able to just write off the top of your head (unless you're taking Creative Writing!). In general, your papers will be based on reading other people's writing and then responding to it. You will need to base your opinions on textual evidence and logical theory.

AUDIENCE

Do you talk differently to your grandmother than you do to your best friend? Do you include the same kind of details when talking to your mother that you do when talking to your significant other? Is your language always the same?

Of course not. That's why it's important to consider the audience of your paper. Consider how different a paper would be if you were writing it for a junior high school audience instead of a college classroom. Think of the differences in tone between writing for an audience of physicians at a doctor's conference and an audience of kindergarten teachers at an education conference.

Make sure you understand the assignment. Ask your teacher questions. Guarantee that you know why, how, and to whom you are writing. Your paper will be improved, and it will be easier to write.

In addition to considering the general audience of the paper, it is also important to ensure that you keep in mind what you are supposed to be writing about when given a prompt. Prompts are always crafted to illicit a specific response. Not that there is only one correct answer, but the topic of your paper should be exactly what the prompt is asking for.

Be alert to the following instruction key words that you may come across in exam questions. If the question asks you to analyze something, it doesn't mean the same thing as if the question asks you to define something. These terms are NOT used interchangeably.

Analyze	examine critically to bring out the essential elements of
Apply	make use of as relevant or to apply a theory to a problem
Assess	estimate, evaluate, or judge the value of
Compare	examine two or more things in order to note similarities and differences
Contrast	compare in order to show unlikeness or differences; to show the opposite qualities of
Define	give the meaning of
Demonstrate	explain or illustrate by example; establish by reasoning
Describe	give a detailed account, list characteristics, qualities, and parts
Determine	decide upon; conclude or ascertain after reasoning or observations
Discuss	consider and debate or argue the pros and cons of an issue. Compare and contrast
Distinguish	indicate or show a difference between
Enumerate	list several ideas, aspects, events, things, qualities, reasons, etc.
Explain	make clear the cause or reason of; to make known in detail
Generalize	form a general opinion or conclusion from only a few facts or cases
Illustrate	give concrete examples; explain clearly by using comparisons or examples

Interpret	comment upon, give examples, describe relationships; describe, then evaluate
Justify	show or prove to be just, right or reasonable
List	items written in a series that creates meaningful grouping or sequence
Outline	describe main ideas, characteristics or events (different from a Roman numeral/letter outline)
Prove	support with facts
Rank	make order arrangements of items
Show	explain what is meant
Summarize	write a brief and comprehensive recap of previously stated statement

DETAIL

Whenever possible, use SPECIFIC details instead of GENERIC ones. College composition students often write too little, putting forward the briefest possible descriptions instead of details which create a picture for the reader. Remember that the readers of your paper do NOT have the ideas or experience that you have and can't possibly know what you're thinking unless you tell them.

Consider the difference in these two passages which discuss the early morning surroundings on a country farm:

"The morning dew glistens like thousands of diamonds decorating each finger of grass. Trees bask their leaves in the remnant of starlight, and somewhere a hoot owl calls. Embryonic beginnings of a sunrise in barely visible shades of lavender can be discerned just above the horizon."

"It's morning and the dew is on the grass. Trees stand in the last of the starlight, and somewhere a hoot owl calls. You can barely see the sun as it comes up."

Of course, some assignments call for technical, concise sentences, but many more assignments benefit from the addition of specific details which utilize the senses of taste, touch, sight, sound, and smell.

Of course, sensory details are not the only important details to consider in an essay. Even when a more technical paper is being written, the more precise and detailed it can be (without sacrificing conciseness) the better. Consider the following example. Imagine that someone has just taken their car to the mechanic after it broke down, and is leaving a note for their spouse to tell them what happened:

BAD:	The mechanic said the truck isn't working.
OK:	The mechanic said that the truck's engine isn't working.
BETTER:	The mechanic said that the truck's engine broke because we forgot to change the oil.
BEST:	The mechanic told us that the truck's engine isn't working because we neglected to change the oil, and now the engine will need to be replaced.

The more detail that is put into the sentence, the clearer and more useful it becomes. This is the case with all writing.

NO:	The secretary went to file some paperwork.
YES:	The secretary went to file the man's I-9 tax information that he had just filled out.
NO:	The school should be closed down because it is not safe.
YES:	The school should be closed down because there is lead paint on the walls and it is not safe for the children to be there.

CONSISTENCY OF TOPIC FOCUS

"Consistency of topic" really just means that you have to stay "on target." From the time you present your "thesis" (which we'll discuss shortly), to the time you espouse your conclusion, you MUST show the reader how one paragraph is related to another. You need to tie together your thesis to each paragraph, and connect each paragraph to another. Some instructors call this "tying together," this obvious "connectedness" between points as "cohesion" or "cohesiveness."

Cohesiveness happens when you effectively utilize transitions between paragraphs or between sentences.

Typical transitions include the following words and phrases:
Again, also, anyway, as a result, as soon as, besides, certainly, even though, finally, for example, furthermore, granted that, however, in addition, in conclusion, in the mean-

time, indeed, instead, likewise, moreover, nevertheless, of course, on the other hand, otherwise, therefore, even though.

Another strategy to create consistency and cohesion is to use sequential words. For instance, if you are discussing the three main reasons that students cut classes, you might introduce your evidence with words like, "First and foremost," "Secondly," and "The third reason…."

TIP: Many students seem to fear the written word, using as few words as possible in a paper. Don't be afraid to verbally explain your thought progression. Transitions can, after all, be more than just a word or a phrase. Good transitions can be entire sentences that explain to the reader where you're taking them. It's okay to say things like, "Even though that's a strong point, there's another more convincing piece of evidence to prove my argument." Sentences like this hold all your paragraphs together and make the argument easier to follow and more logical for the reader who doesn't already know what you think.

MAIN IDEA/THESIS STATEMENTS

All writing is done for a reason: to prove a point, to give information, to influence a decision. Whatever the main idea of the paper is, it should be clarified. Your writing will also be improved if you know exactly what you're trying to do. (You'd be surprised how many college students just begin to "write," without ever understanding what it is that they need to accomplish by writing.)

An excellent place to insert your thesis is at the end of the introductory paragraph. Notice in the paragraph below how easy it is for the reader to get involved with the topic through the introductory material and know what the writer hopes to accomplish:

> "It all started when I read that mysterious, taunting, opening line: "Last night I dreamed again I went to Manderly." From the time years ago when I immersed myself in REBECCA'S English estate filled with writing desks, chintz, flowers, and silver serving trays, I developed a craving for the hot, soothing, golden-topaz elixir called tea."

As a reader, you can surely tell that this article is about TEA. Remember that thesis statements don't have to be boring. Granted, in some academic writing the thesis statement will be drier or more direct than in others, but you can retain flair and still make an obvious statement about the purpose of the article.

EVALUATION OF AUTHOR'S AUTHORITY AND APPEAL

In order for your writing to have "authority," or "credibility," you must present logical evidence. As mentioned in Part I of this guide, the writing you will do in College Composition is usually based on outside sources, and rarely on your own opinion.

To give your own writing authority, you need to show that you've done your research, citing experts, statistics, quotes, or anecdotes.

"Appeal" can mean two things:
1) An earnest or urgent request
   The local police station might appeal to the local high-school students in an effort to stop drinking and driving.
2) The power of attracting or of arousing interest
   The speaker appealed to the sense of fairness the listeners displayed and won their confidence.

To give your writing "appeal," you need to understand the audience, tone, and purpose of the assignment. If you know who you're talking to, and you know what you're trying to accomplish, and you understand WHY you're writing at all, you've mastered the art of "appeal."

But "appeal" isn't just an aspect of your own writing. It can also be used to evaluate outside sources. For instance, if you ascertain WHY an author is writing an article, you may more easily evaluate the validity of his claims. Beware of articles that are biased from the beginning. For instance, if a staunch supporter of gun use who is a member of the National Rifle Association is writing about the safety of guns, he will probably filter or not present information that suggests that guns are dangerous. Chances are, he'll appeal to your emotional sense of freedom and "the right to bear arms."

On the other hand, someone who has experienced great tragedy due to the use of illegal firearms will filter out or not present information that demonstrates safe use of guns and will appeal to your emotional sense of fear. Whatever the argument, pay attention to the authority and the appeal of the author in order to evaluate the validity of the article.

STRATEGY FOR WRITING THE ENTIRE ESSAY

Take a look at this online writing assistant site for essays http://www.powa.org/

1. Make sure your first paragraph contains your thesis statement. A thesis is a sentence that states the main point or idea of the essay. The thesis will give your essay direction. If the essay topic is controversial, the first paragraph is also where you will either agree with or disagree with the statement. In both cases,

you will have to use supporting evidence. The side you choose has nothing to do with the score you receive. You will be scored on your ability to organize and write effectively.

2. Think of at least three supporting factors for your thesis and expand on those ideas with examples or illustrations. Each supporting factor should have its own paragraph. Use the scratch paper provided to write outlines or ideas.

   Useful transitions to illustrate an idea: For example, To illustrate, For instance, In this manner, In particular, Thus.

3. The last paragraph will be your conclusion. Your conclusion will be a summary of the points you have made on your thesis. Do not add a new idea in your conclusion. This is the time to give your essay positive closure with the last sentence. The reader, in this case the grader, should not feel abandoned in the last paragraph. Don't give your essay that dreaded unfinished feeling. The thesis gives your paper direction, but it has to end smoothly too.

   Useful transitions for your conclusion: In short, On the whole, To conclude, In brief , To sum up

4. It is easy to get off the subject of your thesis. Make sure you stay on track by reading your thesis after you write each paragraph.

5. The organizational style of your essay should be uncomplicated and straightforward.

6. If you have time, reread the paper when you are finished to look for:
   - Misspelled words
   - Omitted words
   - Incorrect grammar and punctuation
   - Incorrect dates and figures

5 X 5 PARAGRAPH ESSAY

A 5x5 paragraph essay is one of the most basic forms of essay writing. It breaks the essay down into five sections: the introduction, three body paragraphs and the conclusion. Each section should contain five sentences. For the introduction paragraph, the first line should be the thesis. The thesis is followed by three supporting statements, and the final line leads into the next paragraph. The three body paragraphs all follow the same format, with the first line taken from the supporting statements from the introduction paragraph (the first supporting statement starts paragraph two, the second starts paragraph three and the third starts paragraph four). Each body paragraph should then contain three supporting statements and a concluding line which links to the next paragraph. The concluding paragraph should start with a line summarizing the point of the essay, have three sentences restating the original supporting lines and then restate the thesis.

SECTION 4 EXAMPLE: 5X5 ESSAY OUTLINE

5X5 ESSAY OUTLINE

TOPIC:

Introduction

Thesis:_____

Supporting Statement 1 (SS1): _____

Supporting Statement 2 (SS2): _____

Supporting Statement 3 (SS3): _____

Concluding sentence: _____

Body Paragraph 1

SS1:_____

Evidence: _____

_____

_____

Concluding sentence: _____

Body Paragraph 2

SS2:_____

Evidence: _____

_____

_____

Concluding sentence: _____

Body Paragraph 3

SS3:_____

Evidence: _____

_____

_____

Concluding sentence: _____

Conclusion

Summary: _____

Restate SS1: _____

Restate SS2: _____

Restate SS3: _____

Restate Thesis: _____

5X5 ESSAY OUTLINE (SAMPLE)

TOPIC: SCHOOL UNIFORMS

Introduction-

Thesis: All schools should institute uniform policies.
Supporting Statement 1 (SS1): Uniforms foster a sense of identity in schools.
Supporting Statement 2 (SS2): Uniforms ensure that students dress appropriately.
Supporting Statement 3 (SS3): Uniforms increase security.
Concluding sentence: For each of these reasons, uniform policies would make schools more efficient and safe.

Body Paragraph 1-

SS1: Uniforms foster a sense of identity in schools.
Evidence: Many students who cannot afford name-brand clothing may be ostracized.
If students must all wear the same clothes it will decrease feelings of isolation and ensure that all of the students feel like they fit in.
Students will also have an increased sense of community and belonging to the school.
Concluding sentence: Uniform policies would make schools more efficient and safe.

Body Paragraph 2-

SS2: Uniforms ensure that students dress appropriately.
Evidence: For many students clothing is a way to express themselves, and in some cases this can be taken to offensive or inappropriate extremes.
Uniforms are not much different than standard dress codes, and ensure that all students are adequately covered and in appropriate clothing.
If students are in uniform then it is easy to monitor violations which are distracting or offensive.
Concluding sentence: The uniform policy is therefore necessary to ensure that appropriate clothing is worn in schools.

Body Paragraph 3-

SS3: Uniforms increase security

Evidence: Dangerous situations can arise when people are at the school who should not be.

Wearing uniforms allows administrators to easily identify these individuals.

Concluding sentence: Uniforms can be instrumental in increasing safety for students

Conclusion-

Summary: There are many reasons uniform policies should be used.

Restate SS1: Uniforms foster a sense of identity in schools.

Restate SS2: Uniforms ensure that students dress appropriately.

Restate SS3: Uniforms increase security.

Restate Thesis: All schools should institute uniform policies.

5X5 ESSAY (SAMPLE)

TOPIC: SCHOOL UNIFORMS

School uniform policies should be instituted in all schools. For one thing, uniforms foster a sense of identity in schools. They also ensure that students dress appropriately. Furthermore, uniforms increase security. For each of these reasons, uniform policies would make schools more efficient and safe.

One important reason for instituting uniform policies is that uniforms foster a sense of identity in schools. Many students cannot afford name-brand clothing, and may be ostracized for this reason if students are allowed to wear any clothes they wish. Also, if all students are wearing the same clothing, no student will feel isolated or left out because of their clothing. Furthermore, wearing uniforms will give students a sense of community and loyalty to the school and to each other. Therefore, uniforms are a good idea because they will generate a positive atmosphere.

A second reason that uniform policies should be instituted is that uniforms ensure that students dress appropriately. Clothing is often cited as a way for students to express themselves; however, in some cases this can be taken to offensive or inappropriate extremes. If students are required to be in uniform then it is easier to monitor violations, and students will not be confused as to what the clothing standards are. In this sense, uniform policies are not that much different than simple dress codes that are already enforced in schools. The uniform policy is therefore necessary to ensure that appropriate clothing is worn in schools.

Finally, uniform policies should be instituted because uniforms increase security. It is dangerous for both students and faculty when people are on school property when they do not belong there. If students are required to be in uniform it makes intruders immediately identifiable. Furthermore, if teachers and administrators are similarly required to adhere to a dress code, adult visitors would also be easily identified and monitored. Therefore, uniforms can be instrumental in increasing safety for students.

In conclusion, there are many reasons for which a strict uniform policy should be instituted in all schools. Uniforms foster a sense of identity and loyalty among students. They also ensure that students dress appropriately, and give clear and identifiable standards which should be met. Furthermore, they increase security by allowing visitors to be easily monitored. All schools should institute uniform policies.

🎓 *Test Taking Strategies*

Here are some test-taking strategies that are specific to this test and to other tests in general:

- Keep your eyes on the time. Pay attention to how much time you have left to complete that section.
- Read the entire question and read all the answers. Many questions are not as hard to answer as they may seem. Sometimes, a difficult sounding question is asking you how to read an accompanying chart. Chart and graph questions are on SAT tests and should be an easy free point.
- Read the wording carefully. Some words can give you hints to the right answer. There are no exceptions to an answer when there are words in the question such as always, all or none. If one of the answer choices includes most or some of the right answers, but not all, then that is not the answer. Here is an example:

  The primary colors include all of the following:
    A) Red, Yellow, Blue, Green
    B) Red, Green, Yellow
    C) Red, Orange, Yellow
    D) Red, Yellow, Blue
    E) None of the above

Although item A includes all the right answers, it also includes an incorrect answer, making it incorrect. If you didn't read it carefully, were in a hurry, or didn't know the material well, you might fall for this.

- Make a guess on a question that you do not know the answer to. There is no penalty for an incorrect answer. Eliminate the answer choices that you know are incorrect. For example, this could let your guess be a 1 in 3 chance at the correct answer.

What Your Score Means

You are scored from 200-800 in each subject area, reading, math and writing. Your scores from each section are added together resulting in a range from 600-2400. A score of 2400 is considered a perfect score. This study guide is a great way to increase your overall score. If you are ready to focus on a specific area and boost your score, this is the way to do it. Study and practice is really the only way to increase your score.

What is an average score? In 2011, the average scores were: 497 critical reading, 514 math, and 489 writing. Using round numbers, that's about 500 for each subject, about 1500 overall. How does that compare for your Ivy League and local schools?

College	*SAT Critical Reading*	*SAT Mathematics*	*SAT Writing*
Brown University	660-760	670-770	670-770
Harvard University	670-770	680-780	670-780
Texas A&M – College Station	530-650	570-680	510-620
UCLA	570-680	610-740	580-710
Yale University	700-800	700-780	700-790

Don't forget, for admissions, schools look at more than just your SAT scores – but having a great one helps! They look at GPA, courses taken (AP, dual-enrollment, honors), personal essay, meaningful service, school activities, and school involvement.

Test Preparation

This book is much different than the regular SAT study guides. This book actually specifically focuses on an area to boost your scores as high as possible. It teaches you the information that you need to know to improve your score.

We use test questions to test your knowledge and to teach new information. If you don't know the answer to the test question, review the material. This is the best way to target your study to cover the information that you specifically need to know.

To prepare for the test, make a series of goals. Register and plan for the upcoming test. Then decide how much time each day you will schedule to review the information you have already studied and to learn additional material. Take notes as you study; it will help you learn the material. If you haven't done so already, download the study tips guide from the website and use it to start your study plan.

Legal Note

www.ingramcontent.com/pod-product-compliance
Lightning Source LLC
Chambersburg PA
CBHW050351100426
42739CB00015BB/3362